— *Creating* —
SMALL
SCHOOLS

We dedicate this guide to the many teachers, leaders,
and students working to create and sustain excellent small schools.

Dan French ▪ Mary Atkinson ▪ Leah Rugen

Creating
SMALL
SCHOOLS

A Handbook for Raising Equity and Achievement

A Joint Publication

**Center for
Collaborative
Education**

CORWIN PRESS
A SAGE Publications Company
Thousand Oaks, CA 91320

For information:

Corwin Press
A Sage Publications Company
2455 Teller Road
Thousand Oaks, California 91320
www.corwinpress.com

Sage Publications India Pvt. Ltd.
B 1/I 1 Mohan Cooperative Industrial Area
Mathura Road,
New Delhi 110 044
India

Sage Publications Ltd.
1 Oliver's Yard
55 City Road
London EC1Y 1SP
United Kingdom

Sage Publications Asia-Pacific Pte. Ltd.
33 Pekin Street #02-01
Far East Square
Singapore 048763

Printed in the United States of America

Library of Congress Cataloging-in-Publication Data

French, Dan.
Creating small schools: A handbook for raising equity and achievement/Dan French, Mary Atkinson, and Leah Rugen.
    p. cm.
Includes bibliographical references and index.
ISBN 978-1-4129-4177-8 (cloth)
ISBN 978-1-4129-4178-5 (pbk.)
    1. Small schools—United States—Handbooks, manuals, etc. 2. School size—United States—Handbooks, manuals, etc. 3. Education, Secondary—United States—Handbooks, manuals, etc. I. Atkinson, Mary, 1951- II. Rugen, Leah. III. Title.
LB3012.5.F74 2007
371.01—dc22

2006102695

This book is printed on acid-free paper.

07   08   09   10   11   10   9   8   7   6   5   4   3   2   1

Acquisitions Editor:	Rachel Livsey
Editorial Assistant:	Phyllis Cappello
Production Editor:	Beth A. Bernstein
Copy Editor:	Glenn Wright
Typesetter:	C&M Digitals (P) Ltd.
Proofreader:	Dennis Webb
Indexer:	Sylvia Coates
Cover Designer:	Monique Hahn
Design Manager:	Rose Storey

Contents

4. Building Partnerships to Sustain Small Schools 77

PART II: LEARNING AND
ACHIEVEMENT IN EACH SMALL SCHOOL

**5. Teaching, Learning, and Assessment
for High Achievement for All Learners** 97

Preface

The purpose of this guide is to provide educators and community members with a practical overview of all the facets of creating small schools in a district. As staff members of a lead organization in the small schools movement, the Center for Collaborative Education (CCE), we looked for resources to guide schools and districts through the complex process of small school development, and found there were few. We decided we could add to the resource base by developing this guide ourselves, drawing on our own experience and the research and experience of the wider educational community.

Creating Small Schools provides an introduction to and overview of the small schools movement, answering the question, *Why small schools?* It provides lessons and case studies from the field, as well as practical tools and advice for getting small schools started in a district. In the guide, we address different approaches to small school development—from starting new schools in new facilities to converting large schools into clusters of small ones. A centerpiece of the guide is a close look at building partnerships, particularly the importance of district-union collaboration in the creation of small schools.

We highlight the work of the Boston Pilot Schools and the pilot school model as an example of an effective small schools strategy. In particular, the pilot school model demonstrates the importance of giving small schools autonomy over their budget, staffing, schedule, governance, and curriculum and assessment. It is through such autonomy that small schools are able to transform teaching and learning and enable their students to succeed.

The guide also provides a framework and tools for making each small school a place of learning and achievement. Chapters on teaching and learning, school structures, a culture of adult learning, and the practice of collaboration are full of lessons and tools to help small school faculties and leaders build an excellent school. Each chapter contains vignettes that illustrate aspects of the work of small schools development. At the end of each chapter are tools to help schools implement the strategies discussed in that chapter.

While the guide can play an important role in this process, it should be used as part of a larger planning and professional development process for small school design that includes technical assistance and coaching, network meetings, summer institutes, and other support.

Conditions, Principles, and Autonomies for Successful Small Schools

FOUR CONDITIONS NECESSARY FOR SUCCESS

1. **Smallness**—Schools are small and personalized.
2. **Unifying Vision**—Schools have a unifying vision, framed around principles of effective teaching and learning.
3. **Autonomy**—Schools have the autonomy to use their resources to best meet students' needs.
4. **Accountability**—Schools are held accountable for the quality of the education they provide to students.

Small Schools Principles*

Equity and Access—Raise learning and achievement of all students.

Habits of Mind—Teach children to use their minds well.

Personalization—Teachers and students know each other well. There are lower student-teacher ratios so faculty works with fewer students.

Less Is More—Students master a limited number of essential skills and areas of knowledge.

Student-as-Worker, Teacher-as-Coach—Learning is purposeful, meaningful, and related to the real world.

Assessment by Exhibition—Students demonstrate mastery of competencies in multiple ways.

High Expectations, Trust, Respect, and Caring for All—The school culture is built on these values.

Professional Collaboration—The principal and teachers serve multiple obligations and collaborate for the achievement of all community members.

Flexibility, Autonomy, and Shared Governance—Schools have control over their resources.

Five Areas of Autonomy

Staffing—Schools have freedom to hire and excess their staff.

Budget—Schools have discretion in spending a lump-sum per-pupil budget.

Curriculum and Assessment—Schools have freedom to structure curriculum and assessment to best meet students' needs.

Governance and Policies—Schools create their own governance structure and set their own policies.

School Calendar—Schools have freedom to set the schedule for school days and calendar years for both faculty and students.

SOURCE: *These principles are included here with the permission of the Coalition of Essential Schools. The complete material from the Coalition can be read at the Web site http://www.essentialschools.org

Acknowledgments

We would like to acknowledge the many CCE staff who contributed to the development of this guide, as well as staff whose daily work in the schools supports their ongoing improvement: Meg Anderson, Amy Bayer, Annemarie Boudreau, Christina Brown, Peggy Burke, Mary Cavalier, Helenann Civian, Arnold Clayton, Judith Collison, Frank DeVito, Mary Doyle, Joseph Edwards, Robert Frank, Sara Freedman, Karen Hartke, Kevin Keaney, Meenakshi Khanna, Dawn Lewis, Ben Lummis, Jordan Naidoo, Jeremy Nesoff, Martin O'Brien, Jayne Ogata, Monique Ouimette, Meg Robbins, Ruth Rodriguez, Reza Sarkarati, Lynn Stuart, LaDawn Strickland, Jeanne Sturges, Steven Strull, Rosann Tung, Dania Vazquez, Beatriz McConnie Zapater.

Corwin Press gratefully acknowledges the contributions of the following reviewers:

Michael Klonsky
Director
Center for Innovative Schools
Chicago, IL

Don Shalvey
CEO and Co-Founder
Aspire Public Schools
Oakland, CA

Sue Showers
Director of Small Schools
West Clermont School District
Cincinnati, OH

We are grateful for the generous contribution from the Bill and Melinda Gates Foundation, which helped support the creation of this guide.

About the Authors

 **Mary Atkinson** has over twenty-five years of experience in education as a teacher, curriculum consultant, and writer. She has worked both as an elementary Spanish bilingual teacher and a Spanish language teacher for grades K–12. She cowrote the Massachusetts World Languages Curriculum Framework and wrote the Texas Framework for Languages Other Than English. As a consultant to the Center for Collaborative Education, Ms. Atkinson was lead author of several Turning Points guides as well as this handbook. Her poetry and fiction for children has appeared in several books and magazines. Ms. Atkinson holds an MEd from Lesley University.

 **Dan French,** executive director of the Center for Collaborative Education, is the former director of instruction and curriculum for the Massachusetts Department of Education and a special educator. He holds an EdD from the University of Massachusetts at Amherst. He has published many articles, including the 1998 *Phi Delta Kappan* article, "The State's Role in Shaping a Progressive Vision of Public Education," and a commentary in *Education Week*, "Boston's Pilot Schools: Progress and Promise in Urban School Reform" (April 19, 2006).

Leah Rugen, publications director, has worked at the Center for Collaborative Education since 1997 as writer, change coach, and program director of the national Turning Points network. Prior to working at CCE she worked for Expeditionary Learning Outward Bound and the New York City Outward Bound Center. She began her education career teaching English and writing in public school in New York. She received her MAT in English from Brown University. Her CCE publications include Turning Points guides *Creating Partnerships, Bridging Worlds: Family and Community Engagement* (with Jordan Naidoo, 2003) and *Understanding Learning: Assessment in the Turning Points School* (2005).

PART I

Creating Small Schools

Key Components of Successful Small Schools

It is with our peers that we will ultimately find our voice and change our world. It is in community that our lives are transformed. Small groups can change the world.

—Peter Block

Two years ago, approximately 29 percent of the students at Central High School were dropping out before receiving a high school diploma, and daily absentee rates ran at about 20 percent. When state-mandated assessments were administered, 80 percent of the student body of 1,400 failed some portion. Students reported that they didn't feel safe at Central; educational materials such as textbooks, computers, and lab equipment were in insufficient supply; and parts of the building were in desperate need of repair. Students did not have equal access to challenging learning opportunities, creating wide disparities in achievement among groups; for example, African Americans and Latinos were three to four times less likely to be enrolled in Advanced Placement courses than were White students.

WHY SMALL SCHOOLS?

Like Central High School, many communities have been plagued by high dropout rates, increased school violence, declines in student learning, inadequate resources, and unequal access to challenging learning opportunities for all students. With high-stakes testing a prerequisite for high school graduation, many schools are confronting these long-term problems and seeking solutions with renewed vigor. Research indicates that large comprehensive schools, especially those serving high percentages of low-income students and students of color, need a radical overhaul if they are to be successful in raising and sustaining achievement for all students.

Educational equity is today's most crucial civil-rights issue. Progress in raising student achievement has been incremental on virtually every measure of student engagement and performance, particularly for Black, Latino, and low-income students. Many touted examples of reducing educational disparity for these groups—the Houston, Texas, school system, for example—have masked the deleterious effects of high-stakes tests on dropout and suspension rates, special-education placement, and grade-retention rates for the very students that these initiatives purport to be helping. Cultures of low expectations, negative stereotyping, and inadequate resources continue to plague public schools enrolling high percentages of Black, Latino, and low-income students. Yet, these very schools are increasingly constrained in their practices through the heavy hand of the No Child Left Behind Act.—Dan French, executive director, Center for Collaborative Education, Boston, MA

Such a radical overhaul must go beyond individual reforms like block scheduling, interdisciplinary curriculum development, and even high-stakes testing. These, and other reforms, when implemented in isolation, have had little impact on raising student achievement.

Many comprehensive high schools are choosing to form small learning communities rather than small, autonomous schools. While the trend toward small learning communities (SLC) within large comprehensive high schools may assist in creating more personalized learning cultures, much recent research points to pitfalls of SLCs that minimize their benefits. For example, a recent report by Jobs for the Future found the following:

- Small learning communities are often layered onto the existing organizational structure of large comprehensive high schools, making an already complex organization even more complex.
- In the layering model, faculty have multiple affiliations—to the SLC and to departments, for example. Students attend and teachers teach classes in both their SLC and the large school.
- The multiple affiliations and choppiness of such arrangements do not offer the heightened accountability for students and teachers that comes from students being known well by a consistent group of adults.

- Because of these pitfalls, "it is unlikely that the positive results associated with being a student in a small, autonomous school will accrue to the students and teachers experiencing such hybrids" (Steinberg & Allen, 2002).

For these reasons, we propose that the best strategy to address systemic public school ineffectiveness is to create small freestanding schools, or to redesign and transform large public schools into small, autonomous schools.

ORIGINS OF THE SMALL SCHOOLS MOVEMENT

The beginning of the small schools movement can be traced to the mid-1970s, when Deborah Meier and a group of like-minded teachers founded Central Park East Elementary School in Harlem, New York. Meier believed that putting an emphasis on the size of the school would success-fully bring the rigor and challenges found in many private schools to stu-dents in low-income communities. New York City became the first urban district to approach the development of small schools as a planned strat-egy for school reform, followed closely by an extensive grassroots move-ment in Chicago. Two decades of subsequent research findings offer compelling evidence about the qualities and conditions of small schools and their effectiveness for improving the education of urban students not well served by large schools.

Small schools developed out of the fairly simple concept that schools ought to be places where each child is known, visible, and valued by at least one caring adult who takes responsibilbity and accepts account-ability for the child's learning. Small schools are an attempt to address sys-temic ineffectiveness through redesigning and transforming large public schools. The small schools movement seeks to improve dramatically edu-cational experiences and outcomes for students and their families. In recent years several foundations, most notably the Bill and Melinda Gates Foundation and the Carnegie Corporation, have moved the small high schools strategy into the public spotlight through significant funding ini-tiatives. This has led to a substantial expansion of small, start-up high schools and the conversion of large, comprehensive high schools to mul-tiple small schools and small learning communities.

Backed by research and a desire to improve conditions for student learning so that all students may participate fully in our democratic society, many large urban districts such as Philadelphia, Boston, San Francisco, Seattle, and Oakland have joined New York City and Chicago in this movement to create a new vision of public education. This vision calls for maximum autonomy and flexibility in small schools planning and implementation in exchange for strong accountability to ensure that all reform efforts are successful in raising student achievement for underserved students.

A Small Schools Success Story: Boston's Pilot Schools

A central principle of our work at the Center for Collaborative Education (CCE) is that schools have the best chance to successfully educate all students if they are granted autonomy over their resources in exchange for increased accountability, all within the economies of scale of a larger urban district. Boston's Pilot Schools, which CCE coordinates, best represent this concept of schooling. The result of a unique partnership among the mayor, school committee, superintendent, and teachers union, Pilot Schools were created in 1994 to promote increased choice options within the city, largely in response to state legislation creating first-time charter schools and the subsequent loss of Boston students to such institutions.

The Pilot Schools are unique among the nation's urban districts for the autonomy schools exercise over budget, staffing, governance, curriculum, and the school calendar as the result of a teachers union contract. As noted in a Boston Public Schools memo (1995), Pilot Schools were intended "to provide models of educational excellence which will help to foster widespread educational reform throughout all of the Boston Public Schools. Ultimately, we hope to dramatically improve the educational learning environment and thereby improve student performance." Starting with four new start-up schools and one school that converted from a regular school, the Pilot Schools Network has now grown to a total of twenty schools spanning grades PreK through 12 and enrolling approximately 6,500 students, or roughly 11 percent of the total Boston Public Schools' (BPS) enrollment.

At CCE, we serve as the Pilot Schools Network convener and coordinator, providing network schools with coaching, networkwide professional development, advocacy, research, and financial management.

In January 2006, CCE released a study, *Progress and Promise: A Report on the Boston Pilot Schools,* showing that Pilot Schools outpace the district average on all student performance and engagement indicators: they have higher attendance, lower suspensions and transfers, and higher achievement and college-going rates.[1] Pilot high school students have a 94 percent attendance rate as compared to an 89 percent rate for students attending regular BPS high schools; this translates to Pilot high school students attending school an average of two additional weeks per year than their peers attending regular BPS high schools. On the Massachusetts Comprehensive Assessment System (MCAS) tests, Pilot students perform at a higher level than the students districtwide at every grade level tested (3–10), in both English and math, and at the passing, advanced, and proficient levels. And while 79 percent of Pilot graduates are attending college one year after high school graduation, only 67 percent of BPS graduates are doing so.

Pilot Schools achieve these impressive results because they control their resources, which they use to implement effective practices, such as small class sizes, low student-teacher loads, long instructional blocks, time for faculty collaborative planning, increased advisory and student support, and a personalized school culture. These are prime reasons why Pilots have among the highest wait lists for student enrollment of any district schools.

With a commitment to equity for students and families at its center, we propose a model for school change that requires that schools embrace the following four conditions to be successful.

FOUR CONDITIONS FOR SUCCESSFUL SMALL SCHOOLS

1. **Smallness:** Schools are small and personalized so that students and teachers know each other well.

2. **Unifying vision:** Schools have a unifying vision of teaching and learning. That vision binds the school community and drives teaching, learning, and assessment, with the goal of creating powerful learning experiences for every student.

3. **Autonomy:** Schools must have the autonomy necessary to create unified learning communities (i.e., control over budgets, staffing, curriculum/assessment, governance, and school calendar), while also benefiting from the economies of scale that remaining within a large district affords (e.g., transportation, facilities, payroll, legal services).

4. **Accountability:** Schools must be held accountable for the quality of the education they provide to students and for student outcomes, through benchmarks and school quality reviews. Students in effective small schools are held accountable through competency-based graduation portfolios and exhibitions, in addition to mandated standardized tests.

Smallness

Increasingly, evidence suggests that small schools can be a powerful antidote to the failures of our nation's large schools. A comprehensive review of the research on small schools reveals that students in small schools do as well academically as, and often better than, those in large schools. Student attitudes are more positive about school, attendance is higher, dropout rates are lower, there are fewer discipline problems, and students participate more in extracurricular activities. All students have equal access to learning at high levels. Team teaching, integrated curriculum, cooperative learning, and other successful grouping and instructional strategies that are easier to implement in small schools are in greater evidence. Parents are more involved, and teachers report that working in small schools is more satisfying. Most important, research indicates that school size affects student performance, particularly the performance of low-income students and students of color (Cotton, 1996).

This study reaches the following important conclusions about small schools:

- Small schools perform at least as well academically as large schools—and often their performance is superior.
- Teaching strategies that are linked with higher student performance are more often implemented in small schools.
- Student attitudes toward school are more positive in small schools.
- Small schools experience significantly fewer discipline problems and less truancy, violence, substance abuse, and gang participation.
- Levels of extracurricular participation are higher and more varied in small schools, and students in small schools gain greater satisfaction from participation.
- Student attendance is higher in small schools, while the dropout rate is lower.
- Students' confidence and academic self-concepts are higher in small schools.
- Small schools have a higher rate of parental involvement.
- Teacher attitudes towards their work and their administrators are more positive in small schools.
- Small schools are effective in combating the effects of poverty on student achievement and in narrowing the achievement gap that separates poor students from their affluent peers, as well as Black and Latino students from White students.

In addition to supporting the educational benefits of small schools, recent research challenges the notion that large schools are cost efficient. A 2000 study on high school size in New York City found that "small academies and large high schools are similar in terms of budget per graduate. Because the literature on school size indicates that small high schools are more effective for minority and poor students, the similarity in [financial costs] suggests that policy makers might do well to support the creation of more small high schools" (Stiefel, Berne, Iatarola, & Frutcher, 2000). Factoring in that high school dropouts add significantly higher future costs to society through increased crime, prison, and welfare rates and lower voter participation rates, the economic argument in favor of large schools becomes even less credible.

Unifying Vision

Our work is guided by principles of teaching and learning and a commitment to equity and access for all students. The CCE Small Schools Principles are a local version of the Ten Common Principles of the Coalition of Essential Schools.[2] They grow out of the research that identifies key characteristics of successful schools. These principles provide a vision for effective small schools and guide the reform work in CCE member schools. Small schools can use the principles as a way of focusing their work as they make decisions about school governance and develop the school's vision. They ensure the principles are embedded in the school's curriculum and assessment practices. These principles are also used in annual assessments of a school's progress toward becoming an effective small school.

CCE Small Schools Principles:

1. *Equity and access.* The school's goals should apply to all students, while the means to those goals will vary as students themselves vary. In particular, there should be an explicit goal of raising learning and achievement levels of low-income students and students of color.

2. *Habits of mind.* The school's central goal is to teach students to use their minds well in every area of work they undertake, to the end of becoming responsible members of a diverse, democratic community.

3. *Personalization.* The school is small and personalized, so that teachers and students know each other well. Student-teacher ratios are greatly reduced so that all faculty know their students well, with secondary ratios at no more than 80:1 and elementary ratios at no more than 20:1.

4. *Less is more.* The school's curriculum is driven by the concept of "less is more." Each student should master a limited number of essential skills and areas of knowledge.

5. *Student-as-worker, teacher-as-coach.* The governing metaphor of the school should be student-as-worker and teacher-as-coach. This helps students to take responsibility for their learning. Learning should be purposeful, rigorous, and related to helping students become powerful in the real world.

6. *Assessment by Exhibition.* Assessment should demonstrate what important things students know and can do, as well as where they are in need of more help. Students should demonstrate their mastery of competencies in various ways, including exhibitions and portfolios.

7. *High expectations, trust, respect, and caring for all.* The tone of the school stresses values of high expectations, trust, respect, and caring on the part of all members of the community.

8. *Professional collaborative communities.* The principal and teachers have multiple obligations and demonstrate a sense of commitment to the

achievement of all members of the school community. Teachers work together to create a professional collaborative learning community.

9. *Flexibility, autonomy, and shared governance.* The people closest to students, including teachers, administrators, parents, and the students themselves, are the policymakers and decision makers. This calls for democratic and equitable forms of school governance and facilitative leadership. The school has maximum flexibility and autonomy, enabling decisions to be made as close to the learner as possible.

Autonomy

Autonomy enables a school to build a unified learning community and use its resources in the best manner possible to provide high-quality teaching and learning to every student. Such autonomy comes with the expectation of increased accountability on the part of the school to track and document its progress.

We believe that small schools should be granted autonomy in the following five main areas:

1. Staffing

2. Budget

3. Curriculum and assessment

4. Governance and policies

5. School calendar

Five Areas of Autonomy

1. Staffing: Small schools have the freedom to hire and excess their staff in order to create a unified school community. This includes:
   o Deciding on staffing patterns that best meet the academic, social, and emotional needs of students.
   o Hiring staff that best fit the needs of the school, regardless of their current status (although every teacher hired becomes a member of the local teachers union).
   o Excessing staff (into the district pool) that do not fulfill the needs of the school.

2. Budget: Small schools have a lump-sum, per-pupil budget, which the school has discretion to spend in the manner that provides the best programs and services to students and their families. This includes:
   o Creating a lump-sum, per-pupil budget, the sum of which is equal to that of other district schools within the relevant grade span.
   o Moving the district toward itemizing all central office costs and allowing schools the option to purchase identified discretionary district services and include them in the school's lump-sum, per-pupil budget.

3. Curriculum and assessment: Small schools have the freedom to structure their curriculum and assessment practices to best meet students' learning needs. While acknowledging that all small schools are expected to administer any state- and district-required tests, these schools are given the flexibility to best determine the school-based curriculum and assessment practices that will prepare students for state and district assessments. This includes:

   ○ Freeing schools from local district curriculum requirements.

   ○ Having graduation requirements set by the school, not by the district, with an emphasis on competency-based, performance-based assessments as long as they meet or exceed the district's standards.

4. Governance and policies: Small schools have the freedom to create their own governance structure that affords increased decision-making power over budget approval, principal selection and firing, and programs and policies, while being mindful of state requirements on school councils. This includes:

   ○ Having the school's site council take on increased governing responsibilities, including principal selection, supervision, and firing, with final approval by the superintendent in all cases; budget approval; and setting of school policies.

   ○ Giving the school freedom from all district policies and flexibility to set policies that the school community feels will best help students to be successful. This includes policies on such areas as promotion, graduation, attendance, and discipline.

5. School calendar: Small schools have the freedom to set longer school days and calendar years for both students and faculty. In particular, research supports a correlation between faculty learning and increased student achievement. Scheduling that allows for summer and school-year faculty planning time contributes to a more unified school community and educational program. This includes:

   ○ Increasing planning and professional development time for faculty.

   ○ Increasing learning time for students.

   ○ Organizing the school schedule to maximize learning time for students and planning time for faculty (e.g., longer days Monday through Thursday in order to have half-days for students on Fridays, providing faculty a significant planning and professional development block every Friday afternoon).

SOURCE: CCE Small School Principals is used with permission of Coalition of Essential Schools. Principles based on the ten common principles of the Coalition of Essential Schools. The complete material from the Coalition can be read at the website essentialscholols.org

Accountability

All CCE network schools are expected to document both their practices and student engagement and performance. Often this occurs through a school quality review. The school quality review process is a proactive accountability strategy for ensuring that schools are engaged in quality educational practices that lead to high student engagement and achievement. Periodic school quality reviews demonstrate the potential of thoughtful school examinations leading to improved practice and higher student engagement and achievement. These reviews are based on a set of public benchmarks as to what constitutes the practices and policies of an effective school. They require a process of self-examination, reflection, and assessment on the part of the school and a team of external practitioners, based on the benchmarks, and the synthesis of this self-assessment into a document for public review (often, a school portfolio). This report articulates a set of strengths, concerns, and recommendations, with the recommendations effectively becoming a road map for future school improvement efforts.

LESSONS FROM EXPERIENCE

From our ten years of experience in supporting the creation of the Boston Pilot Schools Network and assisting other districts with conversions from large to small schools, we have distilled some key lessons.

1. Small, personalized schools that have autonomy over their resources can produce high student engagement and achievement. Autonomy over budget, staffing, curriculum, governance, and schedule is critical for creating the conditions in which schools can flourish. The model is built upon the belief that placing our trust and resources in the hands of people at the school level is the best way to create innovative, challenging, and high-performing schools. As one Pilot principal stated, "What every [school] should have are the kinds of conditions Pilots have. That's everything from size and scale to hiring their own staff to instructional flexibility to governance, the works"(Neufeld, 1999). Ironically, this philosophy is the antithesis of the trend of most urban public school districts in response to the No Child Left Behind (NCLB), Act which is to increase centralization through mandated instructional practices, required textbooks, and more frequent testing.

2. Creating autonomous schools requires a transformed district and teachers union partnership. All too often, teachers unions and school districts are pitted against one another, so that little meaningful reform is achieved. The Pilot School model is a partnership of a different sort, one in which each party lets go of historical control over all of the conditions that govern a set of schools. Instead, the district and union work collaboratively to support autonomous schools.

3. Incrementalism does not lead to fully autonomous schools. Autonomy can only be gained by taking the risk to negotiate the full set of autonomies from the start. The Boston Community Leadership Academy case study (see Chapter 3) illustrates the power of giving a school a complete set of tools with which to undertake comprehensive improvement. As other school districts explore replicating the Pilot concept, it is common for them to look for ways to engage in the strategy by stages. We have discovered that seeking a side letter union agreement for rethinking a job description, or a waiver request from a textbook requirement, or permission for a schedule change will not result in attaining the full scope of autonomies, nor does it allow staff to think about how teaching and learning can be fundamentally different. In districts that have tried a slow start or incremental approach, the process has bogged down at the first stage.

4. School-level accountability is a critical piece of the autonomy equation. Autonomy should come with accompanying high expectations. Pilot Schools undertake a five-year cycle of school quality reviews, in which they conduct a self-study based on the Network benchmarks, and then host a three-day on-site review from an external team of practitioners, who submit a report of findings and recommendations to the school district and teachers union. Along with student outcomes, each school is assessed for vision, leadership and governance, teaching and learning, professional development, and family engagement.

5. Vibrant networks of schools can play a powerful role in spreading success and in influencing district practices. The Pilot Schools have collaborated over the years to influence one another's practice, through monthly leadership meetings, spring retreats, annual teacher sharing conferences, study groups, and cross-school visits. The Pilot School strategy has also led to improvements in the Boston Public Schools in significant ways:
   o The Pilot model of competency-based graduation was instrumental in shaping a new BPS graduation policy that provides multiple pathways to graduation, including one that enables a school to create its own path of courses and performance assessments.
   o The Pilot autonomies have informed the creation of a new set of district schools that can seek a policy waiver to advance their teaching and learning agendas.

o The success of the Pilot high schools was an important factor in the superintendent's decision to convert four large BPS high schools to multiple small schools.

6. Third-party intermediaries can provide valuable assistance to a network of autonomous schools. CCE is the convener for the Pilot Schools Network. Serving as a "jack-of-all-trades," CCE supports the Pilot Schools through coaching, professional development, budget negotiations, advocacy, and research.

GETTING STARTED: SMALL SCHOOLS DESIGN AND IMPLEMENTATION

This section of the guide is a road map that may assist districts and schools in planning small, autonomous, and vision-driven schools. Each district will take its unique path to developing small schools, but there are some common elements that all districts should consider. While the steps in this section are presented sequentially, districts may choose a different sequence that suits them. Indeed, some districts may already be well on their way in small schools design and even implementation; this guide can then serve as a checklist to assess progress.

Important Considerations Before Starting

Before you begin the challenging work of either establishing a new small school or converting a large school into small schools, it is important to keep the following considerations in mind.

Be Prepared to Answer the Question, "Why Small Schools?"

As school and district leaders embark on the journey of creating effective small, autonomous, and vision-driven schools, building buy-in among all constituents for the substantial changes to be undertaken is crucial. In order to get the conversation started, leaders must be able to answer for themselves and for staff, parents, students, and community members the question, "Why small schools?" There are three good entry points that can serve to engage the larger community in this conversation:

1. Facilitate a process of articulating a community vision for the education of the students being served, much as the Small School Principles articulate a vision. Through this process, constituents may begin to understand how their desires are best accommodated in small, personalized settings.

2. Build community awareness of the research base demonstrating that small schools are safer, foster better performance by students from all backgrounds, and are more cost-efficient than large schools.

3. Gather quantitative and qualitative data on your own school, along the lines of that cited in the opening vignette of this chapter (e.g., test scores, attendance, enrollment in honors classes). In this way, constituents may find areas for improvement in their own school, and small schools may provide an answer to those challenges.

Ensure Representation of Key Constituencies on Leadership and Design Teams

Small schools cannot be created in isolation from those who will be affected by them. There should be diverse representation of key constituencies on school-level Design Teams. The design of small schools will have greater integrity and strength when crafted with the input of many.

Ensure Regular Communication With and Opportunities for Input From the Entire School Community

Small schools will be successful when they build support among all the constituencies of the school community—faculty, administration, families, students, and the larger community. While representation helps to accomplish this, everyone involved needs to be regularly apprised of the process of small schools development and its benefits and have opportunities to provide input into shaping the evolving models.

The Autonomies Are Crucial to the Success of Small Schools

Smallness enables greater personalization and makes high-quality teaching possible—but small alone is not enough. In order for small schools to attain their individual visions of excellence, they need to have autonomy over critical conditions of schooling, including budget, staffing, curriculum/assessment, governance and policies, and time. This flexibility enables small schools to craft educational experiences that best meet the needs of the diverse students that they serve.

In the End, It Is All About Learning, Teaching, and Assessment

Smallness and autonomies enable schools to focus on the essence of the educational experience for students—learning, teaching, and assessment. Small schools strive to ensure that learning is purposeful, challenging, and has value in the world beyond school. Every student must be

Table 1.1   Small Schools Design and Implementation

At the District Level

- Establish a districtwide small schools Leadership Team to develop a district plan and to pursue small school autonomies.
- Build community support for small schools.
- Develop a district plan for small schools that includes community input.
- Deliver a clear message to the community on the district's plan.

At the School Level

For large school conversions:

Create a Design Team to guide the conversion. Decide on the framework for the small schools (e.g., theme or philosophy), size, enrollment process, and faculty assignment process.

For Small Schools, Either Freestanding or Sharing a Facility

- Create a Design Team for each small school.
- Develop a vision and design for the small school.
- Decide on the enrollment process.
- Decide on the selection/assignment process for the school leadership and faculty.
- Design the governance and leadership for the small school.
- Construct the curriculum, instruction, and assessment.
- Create the schedule and student groupings.
- Design the personalized culture of the school.
- Design the professional collaborative culture of the school.
- Plan family and community partnerships.

engaged in learning experiences that ensure students are fully prepared to be productive citizens in a diverse and democratic society.

Suggested Sequence for Small Schools Design and Implementation

Table 1.1 suggests a sequence for small school design activities to be conducted at the school and district levels. Each step is discussed in detail in the pages that follow.

Steps to Consider in Small Schools Design and Implementation at the District Level

Establish a Districtwide Small Schools Leadership Team to Develop a District Plan and to Pursue the Small School Autonomies

The five areas of autonomy—staffing, budget, curriculum and assessment, governance and policies, and school calendar—are critical to the success of small schools. Each district should create a District Team to pursue these autonomies for the projected small schools. The team should consist of those district staff who have authority over the five autonomies (e.g., budget director, human resources director, curriculum coordinator), teachers union representation, and representation from each of the proposed small schools (or representation from each large school to be converted into small schools). The goal is to gain the same level of autonomy in each realm for each of the proposed small schools in the district. The team will deal with some areas that need superintendent and/or school committee approval (e.g., budget, curriculum and assessment, governance and policies), while others may also need teachers union approval (e.g., some areas of the budget, staffing, and school calendar). The initial autonomies that each small school will receive should be defined by the June prior to a September start-up date.

Questions to Consider:

- Staffing: To what extent will each small school be provided with staffing autonomy to hire and excess staff and to decide on the staffing pattern that best meets the needs of the school?
- Budget: To what extent will each small school be provided with a lump-sum, per-pupil budget over which it has discretion to spend as it sees fit to provide the best services to students and their families?
- Curriculum and assessment: To what extent will each small school have freedom to set its curriculum and graduation requirements?
- Governance and policies: To what extent will each small school have increased governing authority over budget approval, principal selection and firing, and programs and policies?
- School calendar: To what extent will each small school have the freedom to set longer school days and years for both students and faculty, with a particular focus on creating greater time for faculty to meet?

Build Community Support for Small Schools

Small schools are not necessarily what most adults have experienced. Adults are most familiar with the large, comprehensive high school; they may not immediately see the benefits of small secondary schools. The district should have a plan for building community support for small schools. This could include community forums, newsletters sent to families, and business roundtables. The research on small schools needs to be shared in lay terms, and district data revealing that significant student populations are not currently being served well by large schools need to be included.

Question to Consider:

- How will this plan build community support for small schools?

Develop a District Plan for Small Schools

This plan should articulate a rationale, design, and timeline for creating small schools in the district as well as the construct and philosophy of each small school. For large school conversions, the plan should articulate the small schools to be housed within the larger school facility. There should be a defined rollout plan for each of the district's small schools.

Question to Consider:

- Is the plan clear to the public?

Deliver a Clear Message to the Community on the District's Path

In order to build momentum and commitment to the transition to small schools, a strong message needs to be given to the larger school community stating the district's intent to move to small schools (e.g., how many, in which facilities), the reasons why, the plan for district rollout of small schools, and the timeline, as well as a commitment to seek public input along the way. This message is best delivered by the superintendent and is especially critical in building faculty commitment to small schools.

Question to Consider:

- What is the critical message that you want to communicate to the community?

Steps to Consider in Small Schools Design and Implementation at the School Level for Large School Conversions

Create a Design Team to Guide the Conversion

This team should comprise representative faculty constituencies in the school, as well as district representation. The team should be responsible for deciding how many small schools there will be, the size of each small school, the student enrollment process, and the faculty selection/assignment process.

Questions to Consider:

- Design Team composition: Whom will the Design Team consist of? What constituencies will be represented? How big will the team be? How will members be selected?

- Role of the Design Team: What will be the charge of the Design Team (e.g., developing a design framework for breaking down a large school into smaller schools)?
- Communication and involvement with key constituencies. Who are the key constituencies that need to be kept informed and have opportunities for input? How will you ensure that these constituencies are regularly informed about the Design Team's progress? At what key junctures will you gain their input, and how will you do this?
- Timeline: What is the timeline for developing the design plan? For gaining input from key constituencies?
- Design framework: How many small schools will there be? What will be the size of each small school?
- Student selection: What will be the student selection process for each small school to ensure equitable enrollment across race, income, gender, special education status, and achievement? What will be the faculty selection/assignment process for each small school, to ensure each small school has a core group of faculty committed to the vision of their particular small school?

Steps to Consider in Design and Implementation for Small Schools, Either Freestanding or Sharing a Larger Facility

Create a Design Team for Each Small School

Each small school to be created should have a Design Team that guides the design phase through to the launching of the small school. This Design Team should consist of the new small schools leader, faculty who will be working in the small school, and prospective parents and students. Ultimately, the team should have 10–15 members. The Design Team is responsible for guiding all aspects of small school design through to implementation (e.g., vision, governance, teaching and learning, professional support, family and community partnerships).

Questions to Consider:

- Design Team composition: Who will the Design Team consist of?
- What constituencies will be represented? How big will the team be? How will members be selected? Are members of the Design Team automatically members of the new small school (in most cases, they should be)?
- Role of the Design Team: What will be the charge of the Design Team (e.g., developing a design for a designated small school within a large building, developing a design for a small, freestanding school)?

What are the parameters of the Design Team's task (e.g., is their role completed once the design is finished and approved)?

- Communication and involvement with key constituencies: Who are the key constituencies that need to be kept informed and have opportunities for input? How will you ensure that these constituencies are regularly informed about the Design Team's progress? At what key junctures will you gain their input, and how will you do this?
- Timeline: What is the timeline for establishing the Design Team? For developing the design plan? For gaining input from key constituencies?

Develop a Vision and Design for the Small School

Each small school should have a coherent, well-articulated vision of what the school represents and what students are expected to achieve. The vision should be shaped by and reflect the small school principles and be developed by the planning team with community input. Once developed, it should be manifest in all documents created for the school (e.g., handbook, curriculum guide, orientation material) and be present in the small school's decision-making, policy development, and instructional practices and in other planning.

Question to Consider:

- What is the vision that will drive all aspects of the school?

Decide on the Student Enrollment Process for the School

The student assignment and enrollment process should ensure equitable enrollment by race/ethnicity, income status, language, gender, and special education, resulting in enrollment of these student groups that reflects their relative percentage within the district at each grade level. For this reason, controlled choice, within a ±5 percent range of the district averages for the grade level, is recommended. The enrollment process should include a wide distribution of information about the school so that students and families may make an informed choice about selecting the school.

Question to Consider:

- What student assignment process will be adopted that will ensure equitable enrollment among the small schools?

Decide on the Selection/Assignment Process for the School Leadership and Faculty

Ideally, the school's leadership should be selected by the governing body, with approval from the superintendent. Because this may not be possible in all cases, there should be a process in place that ensures the leadership embraces and is committed to the vision of the school. It is preferable to have faculty voluntarily select the small school in which they will work, while ensuring in large school conversions that each small school receives an equitable distribution of faculty by race/ethnicity, academic discipline, and other local considerations. In all cases, this selection/assignment should be accomplished in concert with the local teachers union.

Question to Consider:

- What faculty assignment process will ensure a critical mass of faculty committed to the school's vision within each small school?

Design the Governance and Leadership for the Small School

Each small school should have a clear governance and leadership structure to guide it. The governance and leadership structure should reflect the principle of democratic decision making and include input and decision-making authority by the full faculty for any significant decisions that affect the small school. The leadership of the school should be clearly delineated—whether it be a principal, director, or teacher-leader. If the small school is located within a larger facility that houses multiple small schools and there is a buildingwide principal or administrator, the relationship between the small school leader and the large school leader should be clearly defined.

In addition, small schools should develop a school governing council and a Leadership Team. The school council governing body should reflect the respective state guidelines for representation (most often administration, faculty, parent, and community representation, and sometimes student representation at the high school level). This body helps guide the school in all phases, and takes on increased governing responsibilities, including principal selection, supervision, and firing (with final approval by the superintendent), budget approval, and setting of school policies. This body usually meets no more than once per month. Each small school should consider having a Leadership Team, a faculty-administration body that meets more often (twice per month) to focus more deeply and in greater detail on guiding the school's implementation in all aspects. The team should be representative of all faculty constituencies. These governance structures should ensure the access of students, faculty, and families for bringing issues forward for consideration, the making of decisions in a timely manner with sufficient input, and effective communication within the entire school community.

Questions to Consider:

- Leadership: What will be the leadership of the school (e.g., principal or some other title)? How will this person be selected? If the small school is sharing a building with other small schools, will there be a building manager, and if so, what will be the delineation of roles between the building manager and the small school leaders?
- Governing body: Who will make up the school's governing body? What constituencies will be represented? How will they be selected?
- Decision making: What will be the shared decision-making structure of the school? What decisions will the school governing body make? The head of the school? The school's Leadership Team? The faculty? Parents? What will be the process for making decisions?

Construct the Curriculum, Instruction, and Assessment for the Small School

This process is at the heart of the small school planning and should include as many faculty that will be teaching in the small school as possible. It is recommended that schools construct their curriculum, instruction, and assessment to be competency based; that is, the goal is to have every student master a set of defined competencies and to demonstrate this mastery in a variety of ways in order to graduate from that school. The curriculum, instruction, and assessment for the small school should be driven by the school's vision.

Questions to Consider:

- Habits of mind: Will the school have overarching habits of mind that drive the curriculum? If so, by what process will they be developed?
- Less is more: How will you construct the curriculum to focus on depth over breadth?
- Student-as-worker: How will the curriculum be constructed to emphasize project-based learning, opportunities for application of learning, and students' engagement in purposeful and meaningful work?
- Assessment by exhibition: What will be the graduation requirements for your school? How will graduation requirements ensure that students demonstrate mastery of key competencies? How will portfolios and exhibitions be embedded in both graduation requirements and the ongoing curriculum?

Create the Schedule and Student Groupings for the School

The schedule and student groupings should reflect the school's vision.

Questions to Consider:

- How will the staff create teams of teachers that are responsible for and accountable to a defined group of students?
- How will the schedule ensure significant common planning time for faculty teams?
- How will the schedule accommodate longer blocks of learning time for academics in order to focus on the principles of "less is more," "student-as-worker," and "assessment by exhibition"?
- Will there be equity in access to a high-quality curriculum for all students and the avoidance of tracking or ability grouping?
- How will staff create student-teacher loads of no more than 80:1 at the secondary level and no more than 20:1 at the elementary level?
- Will there be sustained student-teacher relationships over time— for example, through advisories, looping, and multiage classes?
- Will special education and bilingual/English language learner (ELL) students be included in all classes?

Design the Personalized Culture of the School

A key characteristic of small schools is their ability to create personalized cultures in which each student is known well by at least one adult. This characteristic is one critical correlate to students successfully completing their school career.

Questions to Consider:

- Personalization: How will you ensure that every student is known well by at least one adult over time (e.g., advisories)? What supports will be available for students who need it (including special education), and how will the supports be managed and delivered (e.g., Student Support Teams, learning centers)?
- High expectations, trust, respect, and decency for all: How will you establish a school culture that embodies these values?

Design the Professional Collaborative Culture for the School

There are direct correlations between having a professional collaborative culture that focuses on teaching and learning and seeing increases in student achievement. Each small school should design the structures, schedule, and culture of the school to guarantee significant, sustained time for faculty to meet and discuss teaching and learning and to provide them with the support to learn and practice tools for doing so. For example, small schools may create significant blocks of time weekly for faculty to meet in various groupings—full faculty, academic teams, Critical Friends Groups (CFGs), and study groups. CFGs, facilitated by trained teacher-leaders, meet regularly, with consistent group membership over time, to engage in collaborative practices focused on improving teaching and student learning, including looking collaboratively at student and teacher work, conducting peer observation, and engaging in action research. A formal process for supporting and assessing teacher performance should be part of the professional collaborative culture.

Questions to Consider:

- Professional collaborative communities: What structures and activities will be put in place to ensure the building of a unified professional collaborative community that is engaged in improving teacher practice and student learning (e.g., Critical Friends Groups)? When will faculty meet, how often, and in what groupings?
- Schedule: How will the schedule and staffing pattern be constructed so as to create time for teachers to meet?
- Staffing: What will the staffing pattern of the school look like?

Plan Family and Community Partnerships

Each small school should identify strategies for reaching out to families. These strategies can include involving them in ongoing efforts to improve student outcomes, engaging them in meaningful dialogue about student learning, and providing multiple roles and opportunities for families to participate in the school, particularly in its academic programs and governance. Each small school should also seek to establish substantial community partnerships that support the achievement of the school's vision.

Tool 1.1: Focus Group

Purpose: To begin a discussion about important changes in education over the years, how these changes affect what we want students to know and be able to do, and how small schools can better meet student needs. This tool leads into a "why small schools?" discussion.

Directions: As a large group, answer the following five questions. Each person should contribute. Start with a different person for each round of questions. The facilitator should take notes on chart paper.

1. What are the important changes in our world over the last 25–30 years?

2. What is now most important for our graduates to know and be able to do?

3. How will we know if our students know these things?

4. How would you change schools as they are?

5. How would you involve the community more in our schools?

6. Debrief the focus group. Use these guiding questions:
   • In what ways might small schools address the issues raised in our discussion?
   • What are some next steps our district, school, or classroom should take to move toward our vision?

SOURCE: Courtesy of Tony Wagner, codirector, Change Leadership Group, Harvard Graduate School of Education (http://www.gse.harvard.edu/clg)

NOTE: This activity inevitably leads participants to discussing that schools should be small and personalized.

Tool 1.2: School Visitation Protocol

Purpose: School site visits provide powerful learning opportunities. They enable visitors to create a long-term vision of what an effective school can be like and how it can be achieved. They offer concrete ideas about how good schools work. There are many school visitation protocols available, depending upon the nature and purpose of the visit. This example poses some general questions for small school visitors to consider.

Directions: A site visit to an effective small school should consist of three stages—the pre-visit, the visit, and the post-visit.

1. Pre-visit
   - Plan your visit as a group, even if only one person is to represent the group during the visit. As a group, decide on the purpose of the site visit and create a list of questions you would like to ask and information you would like to collect. You may choose to begin with your own school's strengths or challenges.

2. Visit
   School Climate
   - What is the climate of the school? How are you greeted? Is the physical plant clean and orderly? Are there displays in the hallways?
   - How is the school personalized for students?
   - How do students, teachers, and parents describe the school?
   - How do students interact with other students and adults in the building?
   - How are desks arranged in the classrooms (i.e., rows or clusters)?

   Expectations
   - Are clear expectations known by all? Are they posted in some way?
   - Is student work displayed in classrooms? How are students visible in their work?
   - Are students comfortable asking questions of teachers and other adults?
   - Is there visual evidence of expectations beyond this school?

   Teaching and Learning
   - What does teaching and learning look like in the school?
   - How do students demonstrate what they know, understand, and are able to do?
   - How do faculty work with one another around teaching and learning?
   - What academic support do students who need it receive?

   Facilities
   - How are students using libraries, resource centers, and computer centers during and after the school day?
   - Did you notice anything in particular about common rooms, such as the library, gym, auditorium, and lunchroom?
   - Are computers kept in self-contained labs or in classrooms?
   - In schools that share a building, how do schools divide space between them? How do they share facilities common to the building?

3. Post-visit
    - Ensure that there is a post-visit conversation in which both the host and the visitors participate.
    - Hold your own post-visit meeting at your school to discuss the visit. What was most memorable or impressive about the school? Did you find something you might like to try at your school? Did you notice something you are glad you do not have at your school?
    - Discuss a follow-up action plan for identifying goals.

Tool 1.3: Text-Based Discussion

Purpose: To use existing research to support the rationale for small schools and expand a group's understanding of small schools research in a focused way and in a limited amount of time.

Directions: Follow directions for Tool 7.12 ("The Final Word"), using as a common text a short article about research on small schools. For example:

- Cotton, K. (2001). *New small learning communities: Findings from recent literature.* Portland, OR: Northwest Regional Educational Laboratory. Pp. 13–20. Available from http://www3.scasd.org/small_schools/nlsc.pdf
- Hemphill, C. (2003, October). Why some small schools succeed—and some fail: Lessons from the New York City experience. Available from Insideschools.org Web site: http://www .insideschools.org/nv/NV_small_schools_oct03.php

SOURCE: Used with permission of The National School Reform Faculty Web site www.nsrfharmony.org

NOTES

1. The full report text and an executive summary are available at http://www.ccebos.org/pubslinks.html

2. These principles are included here with the permission of the Coalition of Essential Schools. The complete material from the Coalition can be read at the Web site http://www.essentialschools.org

Launching
Small Schools
in a Community

The Boston Public Schools and the Boston Teachers Union are sponsoring the establishment of innovative pilot schools within the Boston Public School system. The purpose of establishing pilot schools is to provide models of educational excellence that will help to foster widespread educational reform throughout all Boston Public Schools. The parties hope to improve dramatically the educational learning environment and thereby improve student performance. . . . Pilot Schools will operate with an average school-based per pupil budget . . . and will have greatly increased decision-making authority, including exemptions from all Union and School Committee work rules.

—From the 2000–2003 Collective Bargaining
Agreement between the Boston Teachers Union
and the Boston School Committee

NEGOTIATING AUTONOMY: THE ROLE OF TEACHERS UNIONS AND SCHOOL DISTRICTS

Teachers are at the center of creating excellent schools. Teachers are the ones who work most closely with the students. They are able to use both their knowledge of students and the curriculum to shape the day-to-day operations of their small school in a way they know will benefit students. Because teachers play such a key role, they should be included in all aspects of small schools design and implementation from the beginning. Teachers should sit on Design Teams, Leadership Teams, and all committees engaged in developing small schools. In addition, decision-making structures and processes should be in place to guarantee input from the full faculty for all significant decisions. (For more about teacher membership on teams and decision making, see Chapter 7, "Building a Culture of Adult Learning and Collaboration.")

When a districtwide small schools plan is being crafted, teachers unions should be present at all negotiations with the school district. The union helps to plan the district strategy as well as the rollout of specific small schools. This ensures greater buy-in and support for the new small schools.

Successful small schools are granted autonomy over budget, staffing, curriculum, governance, and time. Many of these autonomies require flexibility regarding current teacher contract provisions. For example, creating different staffing roles requires flexibility regarding approved job descriptions. Teachers of history and English may become humanities teachers; a guidance counselor might assume more of the role of social worker. Provisions for teacher seniority may have to be modified in order to allow the hiring of staff who best fit a school's needs and philosophy. Teacher contract provisions on faculty hours and the school calendar might need to be changed to allow small schools to create ample time for faculty collaboration and/or longer blocks of instructional time. Whatever changes need to be made to accommodate the move to small schools, teachers unions must play an integral role. Teachers unions have an important part in the discussion on switching the determination of teacher work conditions from the district level to each small school by framing the contract to allow small schools to create their own work conditions.

Once it is agreed that teacher work conditions are to be established at the small school rather than through the city or town's standard teacher contract, the small school should develop new work conditions through a voluntary work election agreement. The Boston Pilot Schools are an excellent example of a set of schools that, by teachers union contract, establish their work conditions at the school level rather than through the contract. This arrangement for setting work conditions is embraced by Pilot teachers primarily because they have such a prominent voice in decisions made in their schools.

Likewise, there are autonomies that require freedom from school district policies and practices. For example, small schools should be freed from local district graduation requirements as long as their own requirements meet or exceed those established by the district. Often, effective small schools require students to demonstrate mastery over a set of graduation competencies through a series of exhibitions and portfolios instead of passing a certain number of courses. In the budgeting realm, rather than allocating staff positions according to how many students are being served at the school, as occurs in most school districts, effective small schools receive one lump-sum, per-pupil budget for the total number of students being served, and it is then the school's responsibility to determine staffing patterns and resource use. Effective small schools are also able to establish the school's policies over attendance, discipline, and promotion in order to ensure that they reflect the school's philosophy and vision. These are all examples of autonomies that must be negotiated with the district, hence the need for strong district support and buy-in at the start of a small schools initiative.

Granting these district-based autonomies requires new modes of operating for district central offices, in which the central office becomes more of a service provider than the body that sets policy and monitors its implementation. The budget office collaborates with the small schools to develop a lump-sum, per-pupil budget formula that is equitable with the resources that regular district schools receive, and even strives to begin to identify central office discretionary costs that could potentially be added to the lump-sum budget formula (e.g., district-based professional development, literacy and math coaches, textbooks). The human resources office becomes more flexible in assisting small schools to advertise and seek out teacher and administrative candidates through alternative avenues and to craft job descriptions in new ways that reflect the greater personalization that is required of small school professionals. The curriculum office assists small schools in identifying resources that match the competencies, themes, and essential questions that are the framework of their curriculum, rather than distributing the required district textbooks. In each case, the district personalizes its services to meet the unique needs of each individual small school.

ORGANIZING COMMUNITY SUPPORT FOR SMALL SCHOOLS

Community organizing creates the social capital necessary to form equal partnerships between the community and schools. This enables groups to break through bureaucratic paralysis and to generate public demand for policies and resources to eliminate disparities in the education system.

—Bilby, 2002

There is a convincing body of research that supports the correlation between increased community engagement and higher student achievement (Funkhouser & Gonzales, 1997; Henderson & Berla, 1994). Over the last twenty years, school reform efforts across the country have often incorporated measures to enhance community and family involvement. Strengthening family and community involvement must be a continuing priority of a district's small school initiative.

A school's capacity for profound change is intimately linked to the host community's social/political culture—thus any school reform work must be accompanied by a strategy aimed at engaging parents and community. The need to build ownership and support among parents, students, and the school community is an important challenge.

Many communities are unaware of the benefits of small, autonomous schools—and, in particular, their effectiveness in serving low-income students and students of color. From the start, small school Design Teams should engage parents, students, and other members of the school community in the change process in meaningful ways. As school leaders educate themselves about small schools, they should also educate others.

The demands for school reform have often precluded a period of information sharing and data gathering between districts, schools, and their families and communities about how to shape, design, and participate in schools. Overlooking this process can result in conflicts when communities and families "catch up" to reforms. It's never too late or early to begin building new bridges to families and community, to open up the lines of communication, and to develop paths for authentic collaboration.

PRINCIPLES FOR COMMUNITY ORGANIZING

- ***Design Teams should be deeply rooted in the community.*** Identify a group of parent leaders and key community organizations in neighborhoods associated with each prospective small school. Establish alliances with these individuals and organizations, particularly those connected to families of color. Solicit their involvement in developing the school.
- ***Provide leadership training for parents and community organizers.*** Include training on advocacy and community organizing for small schools, parent engagement strategies within these schools, and parent/community representation in shared governance structures.
- ***Assist parents/community members to organize*** so they can increase their involvement in small schools. Enable parents and

others to become involved in publicly voicing their support for the creation of small schools.

- *Assist parent/community leaders in building vibrant community partnerships*. Help parents and community members build partnerships that form the fabric of each small school (through the creation of internships and apprenticeships, learning centers, health and support services).
- *Build support for small schools among civic leaders.* Cultivate relationships with political leaders and other key community members, such as teachers union representatives, school committee members, business executives, and foundation officers, to encourage a positive climate for small schools development.
- *Promote media awareness about small schools and their benefits* by means of op-ed columns and letters to the editor, press releases, and planning media-worthy events.

Sample Community Organizing Activities

The following activities help to inform a wider public about the characteristics and advantages of small schools and to encourage community members to advocate for their creation:

- **Community forums**: Organize community forums to introduce parents and other interested people to the small schools concept.
- **Small schools expos:** Small schools expositions in target communities are major vehicles to convince low-income parents and parents of color to enroll their children in small schools. These events are intended to draw a large audience and might include exhibitions of each small school and presentations by students in existing small schools.
- **Structured visits to existing small schools:** Community members and parents participate in annual structured visits to existing small schools so they can experience firsthand the unique qualities of these schools.
- **Annual conference to highlight successful small school practices:** This event brings together parents and community to highlight successful practices in small schools as well as the work of parent and community organizations in their efforts to create such schools.

PILOT SCHOOL REPLICATION IN FITCHBURG, MA

The first district outside Boston to replicate the full Pilot School model is the Fitchburg (MA) Public Schools (FPS). Located in central Massachusetts, FPS is a small urban district enrolling approximately 6,000 students in prekindergarten through grade 12. The district has rapidly increasing Southeast Asian and Latino populations.

Fitchburg is in the process of creating two schools modeled after Pilot Schools. Fitchburg Arts Academy, an arts integrated middle school, began in September 2006. A feeder high school will begin in September 2008. The schools are a partnership between the Fitchburg Public Schools and Fitchburg Teachers Association (FTA). The new schools share the same five areas of autonomy as Pilot Schools: staffing, budget, governance, curriculum and assessment, and school calendar.

School year 2005–2006 was a planning year to design the two small schools—a middle school of 200 students and a high school of 400 students. Both schools will be arts-integrated schools. In September 2006, Fitchburg Arts Academy (grades 5–8) opened with full enrollment. In September 2007, the Partnership High School (grades 9–12) will open with a ninth grade and add a grade each year until it reaches full enrollment.

A Design Team planned the new middle school, while a Design Team has been meeting for the high school. The team consists of teachers, museum staff, parents, educators, and community members from Fitchburg, as well as educators from other communities interested in developing the schools. Coaches from the Center for Collaborative Education facilitate the team.

THE DESIGN TEAM AT WORK

Beginning in August 2005, the middle school design team met regularly and developed a vision statement for the schools, formed a work timeline and completion list, examined equity, and learned about the features and areas of autonomy found in Pilot Schools. Subcommittees formed to research and develop different areas of the "blueprint" for the schools. The blueprint has twelve sections, ranging from school vision and culture to student assessment to community involvement. Students participated in focus groups to help inform the design team's work. A school visit to Boston Arts Academy, a performing arts Pilot high school, was a critical learning experience for the team.

A Fitchburg Partnership Steering Committee was created to oversee the Partnership Schools and includes the superintendent, assistant superintendent, FTA president and vice-president, chairpersons of the design teams, and CCE staff. The Steering Committee's role is to oversee the planning and rollout of the two Partnership Schools. As part of their responsibility, the Steering Committee has reviewed and approved five middle school blueprints and proposed an election-to-work agreement, which defines the work conditions for teachers who elect to work in the school. The Steering Committee and Design Team developed student recruitment strategies, hired the middle school principal, and conducted an orientation for the community about the new middle school (Center for Collaborative Education, 2006).

Tool 2.1: Excerpt From the Boston
Pilot Schools Collective Bargaining Agreement

The Boston Public Schools and the Boston Teachers Union are sponsoring the establishment of innovative Pilot schools within the Boston Public School system. The purpose of establishing Pilot schools is to provide models of educational excellence that will help to foster widespread educational reform throughout all Boston Public Schools. The parties hope to improve dramatically the educational learning environment and thereby improve student performance . . .

Pilot schools will be open to students in accordance with the Boston Public Schools controlled choice plan. Pilot schools will operate with an average school-based, per-pupil budget, plus a start-up supplement, and will have greatly increased decision-making authority, including exemptions from all Union and School Committee work rules. The actual establishment of such schools will be pursuant to the issuing of Requests for Proposals (RFP). The RFP will be developed and reviewed by the BPS/BTU Steering Committee. No pilot school shall be established without the approval of the Joint BTU/BPS Steering Committee and the School Committee.

Teachers, paraprofessionals, nurses, guidance counselors, substitutes, and all other employees at Pilot schools who fall under the jurisdiction of the BTU contract throughout the school system will be members of the appropriate BTU bargaining unit. These employees shall accrue seniority in the system and shall receive, at a minimum, the salary and benefits established in the BTU contract.

Employees in Pilot schools will be required to work the full work day/work year as prescribed by the terms of the individual pilot school proposal. Further, they shall be required to perform and work in accordance with the terms of the individual pilot school proposal.

Nothing in this Agreement shall prevent Pilot School governing bodies from making changes to their programs and schedules during the year.

All BTU members who apply for positions at Pilot schools shall receive the following information at the time of their application:

- the length of the school day and school year;
- the amount of required time beyond the regular school day;
- any additional required time during the summer or school vacations; and
- any other duties or obligations beyond the requirements of the BTU contract.

BTU members who are employed at a pilot school shall receive, prior to the end of the school year, the same information as stated above.

The Governing Board of each pilot school shall develop an internal appeals process to allow any staff member to raise issues, concerns, or problems. The internal appeals process shall be submitted to the Joint BTU/BPS Steering Committee[1] for approval. The internal appeals process shall be provided in writing to all BTU staff members.

Issues not resolved at the school level may go to mediation under Article X-C of this agreement. Final resolution will be made by the Superintendent of Schools and the President of the Boston Teachers Union. . . .

Employees shall work in Pilot schools on a voluntary basis and may excess themselves at the end of any school year.[2] No BTU member may be laid off as a result of the existence of Pilot schools.

The specifications for the RFP on Pilot schools is agreed to by the parties and is hereby incorporated by reference.

Pilot school positions will be posted on the BPS web page.

New Article III E

1. The parties agree that a minimum of seven pilot schools, provided there are sufficient proposals to consider, will be created through September 2009 under this agreement. The new Pilot schools may result from conversions, newly created schools, and/or charter schools that opt to become pilot schools. There shall be a union-sponsored[,] teacher-run pilot school at the site of the Thompson Middle School, effective 9/2009 or as soon as the Thompson building is available for such use. This school shall be run exclusively by the BTU Bargaining Unit members on staff. This pilot at the Thompson shall be counted as one of the seven schools. Nothing described in this paragraph shall supersede the Contract language found in Article III D, specifically, the language that gives the BTU president or superintendent veto power over any particular pilot school.

2. The parties agree that a teacher work year schedule (including length of work year, length of work day, professional development time in and out of school, and summer work) shall be created by the Governing Board and shall be given to affected staff no later than January 15 of the previous school year. By a 66% (2/3) vote, affected BTU Bargaining Unit staff may vote to override the proposed schedule, sending it back to the Governing Board for possible re-working. If a schedule for an upcoming school year has not been approved by February 15th the previous year's schedule shall remain in place. Staff wishing to excess may do so on February 15th. If after the start of school year, the Governing Board of a pilot school wishes to change must be approved [sic] by a 66% (2/3) vote of the affected BTU Bargaining Unit staff. The following paragraph, currently found in Article III D of the 2003–2006 CBA, shall be deleted: "Nothing in this agreement shall prevent Pilot School governing bodies from making changes to their programs and schedules during the year."

   i. Bargaining Unit members who work in a pilot school shall get paid at the contractual hourly rate for hours scheduled in accordance with the above paragraph as follows: For all hours scheduled in excess of the traditional teacher work day and year (as mentioned in the first sentence in section 2) for their respective school levels (elementary, 6:30 per day: secondary 6:40 per day) of 183 days and 18 hours, the following schedule shall be in effect:

     1. In 2006/2007, excess hours up to 105 per school year shall not be compensated. Compensation for hours from 105–155 shall be paid by the school department. Compensation for hours beyond 155 shall be the responsibility of the individual pilot school.

     2. In 2007/2008, excess hours up to 100 per school year shall not be compensated. Compensation for hours from 100–150 shall be paid by the school department. Compensation for hours beyond 150 shall be the responsibility of the individual pilot school.

     3. In 2008/2009, excess hours up to 95 per school year shall not be compensated. Compensation for hours from 95–145 shall be paid by the school department. Compensation for hours beyond 145 shall be the responsibility of the individual pilot school.

   ii. All pay, regardless of the source of funding, will be annualized and retirement-worthy.

3. [This section deals with Discovery Schools, and is unrelated to Pilot Schools.]

4. The parties agree that there will be established an intervention process that can be invoked under certain conditions to be established. Either party will be able to initiate an intervention process. The process will parallel the process as found in Article IV C of the CBA.

5. Each pilot school's Governing Board shall include no less than four teachers.

6. Disputes over the interpretation or application of Article III E I 1, I 2, and I 3 shall be resolved in accordance with the arbitration procedure, waiving all intermediate steps, of the parties' collective bargaining agreement unless the superintendent and the union president can agree on a resolution.

7. The two Boston Horace Mann Charters, the Boston Day and Evening Academy and the Health Careers Academy, will fall under this newly named Article III e of CBA.

8. Teachers in Pilot schools must excess themselves by February 15 of a given school year. Pilot School principals and headmasters must excess teachers by February 1 of a given school year.

9. The parties agree that sections 2i 1, 2, 3 and section 6, if applicable, apply to paraprofessionals.

10. Article III E in the CBA will be renamed Article III F.

SOURCE: Collective Bargaining Agreement between the Boston Teachers Union Local 66 MFT, AFL-CIO, and the Boston School Committee, effective September 1, 2003, through August 31, 2006, pp. 27–28. Retrieved November 11, 2006, from http://www.btu.org/leftnavbar/contractdownload.html
NOTE: New Article III E was ratified in January 2006.

Tool 2.2: Sample Work-Election Agreement

Election Agreement to Work at Boston Arts Academy

1. I, _____, am voluntarily electing to work at Boston Arts Academy Pilot School. I am signing this Election Agreement to indicate I understand and agree to the following terms and conditions of my employment.

   The Boston Arts Academy Pilot School is supported by the Pilot Schools program described in the Collective Bargaining Agreement between the School Committee of the City of Boston and the Boston Teachers Union (the "BTU Contract") and in the Pilot Schools Request for Proposals which is the document that established Pilot Schools in the Boston Public Schools. Employees of Pilot Schools are to receive salary and benefits as they would at any other Boston Public School, as specified in Article VIII, Compensation and Benefits, and Article III of the Paraprofessional Section of the BTU Contract for their members. Other terms and conditions of employment for BTU Employees will be determined by the Boston Arts Academy Pilot School's administration and the Boston Arts Academy Pilot School's governing body, rather than by the BTU Contract.

   While not attempting to be exhaustive, this Election states the more significant terms and conditions. These terms and working conditions will be subject to change from time to time as the Boston Arts Academy Pilot School may make changes to its program and schedule during the year. These changes will occur with prior notice by the Leadership Team and sufficient discussion in faculty meetings.

2. Salary, Benefits, Seniority and Membership in a Bargaining Unit

   BTU Employees will continue to accrue seniority as they would if they were working elsewhere in the Boston Public Schools. Employees hired as teachers will receive the salary and benefits established in the BTU Contract, Article VIII.

   BTU Employees will be members of the appropriate Boston Teachers Union bargaining units. (Note: No seniority accrues until and unless a teacher is made permanent, and then seniority is retroactive.)

3. Terms of Employment

   Work Day for Academic Years 2005–2006: 7:55 a.m. to 4:00 p.m., Monday through Thursday, and 7:55 a.m. to 3:30 p.m. on Friday. Twice a month, there is a grade level meeting until 5 p.m. There may also be different work schedules for some employees.

   Employees will attend one Friday to Saturday retreat during the year, probably in January. Advance notice will be given. Employees will attend two evening family conferences throughout the school year. Employees will also work occasional additional time determined by each department to provide for student performance and presentation activities.

   It is also expected that all faculty members participate in weekly department meetings and these may extend after school.

Work Year

Prior to the School Year:

The leadership team, with the approval and input of staff, will determine the curriculum and planning workshop dates prior to school. For 2005–2006, these dates are the week of August 29 to September 2.

In 2005, employees will attend and take part in curriculum and professional development workshops and planning. At present, no commitment can be made on stipends for future summers, but efforts will be made to procure funds.

Employees on Salary Plus 10% will work four extra weeks per year, usually two weeks following the end of school, and two weeks before school begins.

Professional days may be scheduled on different days from the rest of BPS.

After the School Year:

All employees will work two days after the end of the BPS year in June reviewing and evaluating year and completing activities.

All terms from the job description under "General description and goals," "Responsibilities," "Terms," and "Qualifications" are incorporated herein for the undersigned employee. This job description can be found on file in the office.

In addition, supplemental hours and tasks necessary to complete the mission of the Boston Arts Academy Pilot School may be required by prior notice of the Leadership Team and sufficient discussion in faculty meetings.

4. Responsibilities

   All responsibilities from the job description under "General description and goals," "Responsibilities," "Terms" and "Qualifications" are incorporated herein for the under-signed employee.

5. Performance Evaluation

   BTU Employees will be evaluated utilizing the standard BPS process (which is currently that provisionals are evaluated annually, and permanent teachers are evaluated every two years) and another process that may be developed by the Pilot School. In the next few years, the Pilot Schools may collaboratively develop a peer evaluation process. Ultimate responsibility for evaluations will rest with the Headmaster.

6. Dispute Resolutions

   The Pilot School will use the Dispute Resolution Guidelines as set out in the BAA's by-laws to resolve disputes where applicable.

7. Excessing

   Permanent teachers may unilaterally excess themselves from the Boston Arts Academy Pilot School at the conclusion of the work year. Similarly, the Boston Arts Academy Pilot

School may unilaterally excess permanent teachers, no later than the BPS deadline for the first excess pool, or at least in conjunction with publication of transfer list at the end of the work year. In the event of such excessing, permanent teachers will be placed on the systemwide excess list, subject to the terms and procedures in Part V. K of the BTU Contract.

8. Dismissal

All employees are subject to dismissal from BPS in accordance with existing law. Additionally, the contract for provisional teachers is limited to one school year of employment.

By signing this Election, I acknowledge that I have read all its provisions, including the attached job description and dispute resolution guidelines incorporated herein, and that I agree to all terms and conditions of employment stated herein.

SIGNATURE:

_____   _____

Name of Employee   Date

Boston Arts Academy Headmaster: _____

NOTES:

1. The BTU/BPS Steering Committee is created through the BTU contract. The committee consists of an equal number of members appointed by the superintendent and teachers union president, presided over by the superintendent and teachers union president. The committee's charge is to oversee implementation of the BTU contract, of which Pilot Schools are one provision.

2. This process must take place within the Voluntary Excess timeline set forth in the BPS Staffing Calendar, which is included in Superintendent Circular HRS-25.

Converting Large Schools to Small

Central High School's Conversion Leadership Team, with input from the entire school community, decided to implement their small schools design by phasing in each of three small schools one grade at a time. In the first year, only the entering ninth graders were placed in the three new theme-based small schools; the upper grades would remain as part of the existing traditional school until they graduated.

Each of the small schools was given a separate section of the larger school. Over time, the larger school would be replaced completely, with the small schools sharing the entire building.

Implementing the small schools design is a challenging undertaking for new start-ups and stand-alone small schools, but the challenges become even more complicated in the conversion of an already existing large comprehensive school. Rather than transforming a large high school into several small autonomous units, schools and districts often simply layer small learning communities onto the existing organizational structure of the comprehensive school. (See below for the differences between small learning communities and small schools.) While small learning communities may overcome, in part, the anonymity and fragmentation of a typical high school structure and schedule, and show improvements in student learning as a result, realizing long-lasting gains in student achievement is more likely in a small autonomous school.

DIFFERENCES BETWEEN SMALL SCHOOLS AND SMALL LEARNING COMMUNITIES

Below are some general characteristics of small schools and small learning communities (SLC). Certainly there can be many variations of each—for example, you can create SLCs that have more of the qualities of small schools than are described below—these descriptions merely provide a sense of the difference between the two.

Table 3.1   Characteristics of Small Schools and Small Learning Communities

Category	Small School	Small Learning Community
Vision	Creates its own unique vision	Shares the large school vision, and may also have an SLC vision.
Budget	Lump-sum, per-pupil budget	Budget allocations in the form of staffing, textbooks, etc., with little discretionary control.
Leadership	Has a principal; sometimes there is also a principal/ CEO who oversees facility operations and coordination among the small schools.	Has a small schools leader who reports to the large school principal.
Staffing	Creates own staffing pattern. Has authority over all staff.	Staffing patterns determined by the large school. Many staff have both large school and SLC assignments. Staff are hired and evaluated by the large school administration.
Governance and Policies	Has its own governance body, which establishes policies.	Governance and policy setting remain with the large school.
Curriculum and Assessment	Has freedom to create curriculum and assessment measures. May negotiate some shared courses with other small schools.	A significant portion of the curriculum and assessment is still shared with the large school.
Students	Students spend all or most of their time in the small school.	Students spend all or most of their time in the SLC in 9th and 10th grades, and an increasing amount of time in the large school in the 11th and 12th grades.

Some large schools engaged in conversion begin with SLCs prior to adopting a small schools model. This process is successful only when the intent to adopt small schools is an explicit goal from the outset, with a timeline set.

The research varies on the outcomes of small schools and SLCs. The data are much more compelling for small schools—they are superior to large schools on virtually all student performance and engagement indicators. The data on SLCs, while showing them beneficial to students, are more varied. The main reason for this finding lies in accountability— the staff in small schools are held more accountable for the success of their students than the staff in SLCs, where there are more shared resources within the large school, thus diffusing adult responsibility.

Table 3.2   Common Conversion Challenges

The conversion process can raise difficult questions about changes in leadership, equitable distribution of staff and students among the new small schools, and the use of school resources. This chart provides a summary of some of these challenges and offers possible solutions.

Common Challenges	*Possible Solutions*
Parent, student, and community buy-in: The need to build buy-in and support among parents, students, and the school community, including the school committee, is an important challenge.	**Community engagement:** From the start, engage parents, students, and other members of the school community in the change process in meaningful ways. As school leaders educate themselves about small schools, they should also educate others. Create and keep revisiting a shared vision for success.
Staff buy-in: Although most teachers become enthusiastic over time about converting to small schools, resistance among a significant number of teachers can hamper progress.	**Communication:** Decision makers at all levels must communicate clearly the expectations and goals for the planned changes and include staff in all major decisions. **Outreach:** Provide outreach to resistant teachers regarding concerns about union rules, sustainability of change, and decision-making power among teachers in small school design.
Equity in student placement: Maintaining representative student bodies in each small school is a key challenge. Student groups can have	**Equitable student enrollment:** Ensure equitable enrollments in each small school by race, gender, income, special education status, language,

(Continued)

Table 3.2 (Continued)

Common Challenges	Possible Solutions
significantly different learning experiences based on which small school they are enrolled in. For example, when conversion results in small schools "tracking" different student groups, such as honors students and the severely disabled, into special programs, unacceptable equity gaps occur.	and achievement level. Allow student choice whenever possible while ensuring equitable enrollments.
Faculty assignments: Allowing faculty to self-select their small schools may result in inequitable staffing among small schools based on experience, expertise, race, and gender.	**Equitable faculty assignments:** As with student assignments, faculty and staff should have equitable representation in each small school by discipline, experience, race, and gender. Allow for choice whenever possible, but ensure equity.

A CASE STUDY OF A LARGE SCHOOL CONVERSION

The superintendent of the Boston Public Schools (BPS) appointed a new principal to take over Boston High School in June 2000. The school was overcrowded and among the lowest performing high schools in the district. The new principal immediately changed the focus of the school from a work-study school with two shifts of students per day to a single, full-day schedule, college preparatory high school, with the goal of improving student performance.

In the fall of 2002, the staff voted overwhelmingly, in the face of a potential closing of the school, to convert to Pilot status and to rename the school Boston Community Leadership Academy (BCLA). Boston High enrolled 650 students when the new principal was appointed. The enrollment for BCLA was intentionally reduced to a small school size of 400 students, through graduation, attrition, and smaller incoming classes.

From 2000 to 2004,[1] attendance increased, suspensions were stable, and transfers out decreased (Table 3.3).

Table 3.3   Student Attendance, Suspension, and Transfer Rates

Year	School	Attendance (%)	Students Suspended	Transfers out of School
2000–01	Boston High	85	19	19
2001–02	Boston High	86	25	17
2002–03	BCLA	88	21	10
2003–04	BCLA	94	18	6

At the same time, pass rates increased for both the English Language Arts (ELA) and Mathematics portions of the statewide MCAS exams. By 2004, more than 80% of students passed the ELA and Math exams.

Graph 3.1   Passing Rates on the MCAS in English Language Arts

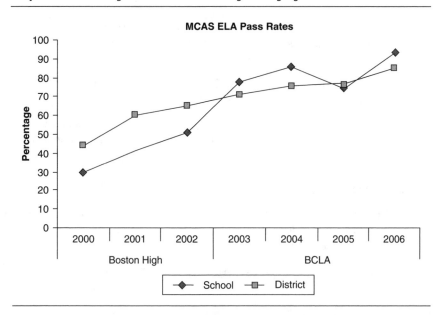

Graph 3.2   Passing Rates on the MCAS in Mathematics

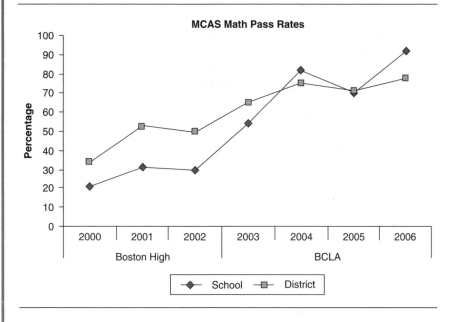

What brought about these positive trends in student outcomes?

Changes in School's Mission

BCLA's new mission statement was created collaboratively by the school Design Team (a group of faculty, administrators, parents, community members, and/or students who submitted the Pilot design proposal) and the staff:

> Boston Community Leadership Academy's mission is to develop the capacity for leadership in all students, empowering them to make a positive contribution to their communities. BCLA's rigorous curriculum prepares students to succeed in college, to lead fulfilled lives, and to participate in our diverse and complex democracy.

> Our vision is to make every student, when they leave us here, not [only go] *to* college, [but] to get them *through* college. —Principal

> I like the [idea] of this school being a college prep [school]. . . . We have a lot more discussions in the classroom, and the teachers are involving every student. So, it's just growing every year, I think, into something good. —Student

Changes in Staff Numbers and Roles

In its first year of operation in 2002–2003, and because of the adoption of Pilot status, BCLA had twenty-four new staff members out of 64, or 37.5% new staff, contributing to a renewal of the school's professional culture.

> With the new teachers, they have created an atmosphere of better expectations. —Teacher

In addition, due to staffing autonomy and greater budget flexibility, there was a focus on decreasing class size: in the first year of Pilot status, the average class size dropped from 28 to 22 students.

> [Before Pilot status,] I had a class that had 28 and there was no way that we could deliver the instruction you wanted to when you have 28 kids in the math class. So we opened another section and asked someone else to pick it up. And you can do all this when . . . you're small and you have that flexibility. —Principal

Table 3.4 Enrollment and Staffing Changes Due to Pilot Status

Enrollment and Staffing	2000–01	2004–05
Total student enrollment	627	400
Decrease in student enrollment	N/A	36%
Total staff in teaching, student support, and administrative roles	65	51
Decrease in staffing	N/A	22%
Student:teacher ratio	13:1	11:1
Percentage of staff who were teachers	75%	73%
Percentage of staff who were student support	14%	20%
Percentage of staff who were administrators	11%	8%

The largest staffing change was that a higher proportion of BCLA's staff is now engaged in student support work than was the case at Boston High. Not only is the support staff larger, others in the school have taken on support roles through advisory.

Changes in Leadership Roles and School Governance

Prior to the Pilot conversion, administrators governed Boston High in a traditional way. The principal made most decisions; teachers were given little opportunity for input. Starting with the Design Team's work toward Pilot status in 2001–02, decision making at the school began to involve teachers, students, and families.

New structures include collaborative decision-making bodies, or teams, designed to provide opportunities for staff, students, parents, and other community members to have a voice in decisions. The school's governing board, Leadership Team, and Curriculum Team now make decisions collaboratively. The governing board is responsible for budget and policy decisions, principal evaluation, and community and business partnerships. The Leadership Team is organized to represent each small learning community and academic area, and focuses on teaching and learning matters. The Curriculum Team works with the director of curriculum and instruction to ensure alignment of their goals, projects, and timelines across content areas.

Changes in Use of Teacher and Student Time

In the principal's first year at Boston High, the average length of the school day was 374 minutes, and the time spent on core academic instruction per day was 222 minutes. Currently, the average length of the school day is 398 minutes and students spend an average of 263 minutes per day on core academic instruction. Students are in school and engaged in academics more than they were in Boston High. The teachers' school year differs from the district contract by an additional 27 hours.

Class periods have lengthened from 58 minutes to 109 minutes, with some 53-minute classes. Once a week, students are released after a half-day so that teachers have more time to meet and discuss their work among colleagues.

> I think what is really happening in terms of teaching is just this opening up and sharing practices. I mean, now it's much more reflective. —Teacher

Changes in Curriculum and Assessment

The curriculum at BCLA is now driven by its mission to prepare students to succeed in college. Academic courses are sequenced to provide students with the prerequisites for college, including four years of math. BCLA no longer offers remedial classes, while physics and five AP classes were added to the curriculum. While time for electives has decreased significantly since 2000 in order to create more time for core academics, the number of electives has increased and their content has attracted more interest among students. Advisories now provide one means to achieving greater personalization in the school. Each student was assigned an advisor for two years; the curriculum includes activities for getting to know each other, study and life skills, college preparation, and community service.

> I like the curriculum because . . . we have . . . changed it to make it more rigorous. We went to the national standard of curriculum, which is better [than Boston's]. —Teacher

Table 3.5   Summary of Changes Due to Autonomy

	Pre-Pilot	Post-Pilot
Mission	Work-study	College-preparatory and Leadership
Enrollment	650	~400
Staffing (and Budget) Autonomy		
Number of staff	65	51
Student:teacher ratio	13:1	11:1
Percentage of staff who are student support	14%	20%
Curriculum and Assessment Autonomy		
Remedial track of courses	Yes	No
Advanced Placement courses	No	Yes, 5
Performance assessments	No	Yes, ELA and math, all grades
Courses of choice (electives)	5	16
Advisory class	No	Yes
Governance Autonomy		
Governance model	Principal	Distributed
Teams for decision making	None	Governing board, Leadership Team, and Curriculum Team
Percentage of staff who are administrators	11	8
Schedule Autonomy		
Predominant instructional block (minutes)	58	109
Length of school day (minutes)	374	398
Time on core academic instruction per day (minutes)	222	263
Collaborative planning time per week (minutes)	None	425
Student Outcomes (Equity)		
ELA MCAS pass rate	30% (below BPS average)	87% (above BPS average)
Math MCAS pass rate	21% (below BPS average)	83% (above BPS average)
Graduates enrolling in postsecondary education	55%	75%

Challenges of Converting to Pilot Status

Despite the gains, there are still challenges that face the school as it continues on its journey to becoming a high-performing urban high school:

- Student dissatisfaction with longer school days
- Discussing access and equity with the introduction of more advanced course offerings
- Changing the school schedule and developing an acceptable work-election agreement
- Developing a shared definition and understanding of new teams' responsibilities
- Bringing shared decision making to the student level

SOURCE: Center for Collaborative Education. (2006). *Essential guide to pilot schools: Overview.* Boston: Author.

SAMPLE CONVERSION DESIGNS

There are multiple options for creating new small schools within a large facility. Some schools opt to "redesign all at once," closing the old school in June and reopening with separate small schools the following fall. Others choose to phase in one or two new small schools each year until the entire building is made up of only small schools. Still others decide to phase in the small schools by grades, establishing a new small school over four years with each ninth-grade entering class. Different schools and districts have different needs and goals. There is no "one-size-fits-all" solution to how a school should undergo conversion.

In choosing the best option, multiple decisions will have to be made. How are the identities, faculty, and students of new small schools established? How many schools will be established at a time? How many grades at a time? Where should new small schools develop? Below are descriptions of four sample implementation options with their related advantages and challenges. Sources include the Small Schools Project, Seattle, Washington (http://www.smallschoolsproject.org), and School Redesign Network at Stanford University (http://www.schoolredesign.net).

Implementation Option 1: Redesign All at Once

With this option, a large school is redesigned into several small schools "all at once." The large school ends the school year in June as one comprehensive school and reopens the next fall as several separate small schools. Teachers and students are assigned equitably to each small school. In the first year, each small school would look essentially the same—in schedule, curriculum, student grouping, etc. The identity of each small school would then evolve over subsequent years.

> **Example:** A school of 1,500 students might use this strategy to break into five small schools with three hundred students apiece.

Advantages: This process of creating the new small schools is quick (with the prior year used as a planning year) and might be attractive to schools where the need for change is urgent. It can ensure equity in staff and student assignment. In addition, this approach also has the advantage of not leaving any students or faculty behind as part of a potentially divisive "phaseout." Being quick, the "redesign all at once" option avoids many of the pitfalls of a longer "phase-in" schedule that can lose the momentum necessary to sustain the change. The conversion has the same impact across the faculty and student population. It allows for crossover programs, courses, and services to be implemented, as well as an evolutionary process from SLCs to small schools (i.e., there could be many shared services the first year, phased out over time). The transformation occurs quickly, eliminating the cultural tensions that might occur between students and faculty still in the large school and those in the emerging small schools.

Challenges: Such a comprehensive change in such a short period could result in little buy-in or ownership on the part of both faculty and students. Any significant faculty resistance could impede the conversion. There would be no models of effective small schools already within the facility to learn from. Each small school might not have a unique vision or identity and might simply be a replication of the ineffective large school and its practices. It is likely that it would be a difficult adjustment for upper-grade students, who have been used to being in a large school culture, making it difficult to establish a unique culture and community identity.

Implementation Option 2: Phase In by Schools

With this option, a large school phases in one or two small schools each year, with each small school serving a group of students in grades 9–12. For example, in the first year, two new small schools can be introduced, while the large school still exists in the same building. In subsequent years, the large school's enrollment continues to decline as students start attending the small schools, until the conversion is completed and every student is enrolled in a small school.

> **Example**: A school of 2,000 students breaks into six small schools of differing enrollments during a four-year period.

Advantages: Small schools develop slowly, grade by grade, and become progressively more sophisticated and independent as they grow. Although some existing students may feel left out of the redesign, it allows most to stay with the traditional school they're used to. This model allows a small school to create a new learning culture and vision from the beginning,

Table 3.6 Phase In by Schools

Year 0	Year 1	Year 2	Year 3	Year 4
Grades 9–12, 2,000 students	2 new small schools, with 200 students and 300 students, respectively	1 new small school with 400 students added, for a total of 3 small schools and 900 students	1 new small school with 300 students added, for a total of 4 small schools and 1200 students	Six small schools: 200 students 300 students 400 students 300 students 400 students 400 students
	1,500 students in large school	1,100 students in large school	800 students in large school	

with students and faculty buying into it. It also allows a small school to experiment with its practices and structures (e.g., schedule) to find the most effective ones while working with fewer students. Students accustomed to the large school would not be required to change in midcourse.

Challenges: Since the total conversion takes place over a period of four years, it takes longer for all students to be enrolled in a small school. Faculty and students in the large school and those in the small schools might encounter tensions.

Implementation Option 3: Phase In by Grades

Under the "phase in by grades" option, one or two grades are phased in at a time, starting with the ninth grade and ultimately expanding to include grades 9–12. Each year a new group of ninth graders joins the students already enrolled in the small schools. The upper grades remain part of the current large school until they have graduated.

> **Example:** Starting with the ninth grade, a 900-student school uses this method to break into three 300-student small schools over a four-year period.

Advantages: Small schools develop slowly, grade by grade, and become progressively more sophisticated and independent as they grow. Although some existing students may feel left out of the redesign, it allows most to stay with the traditional school they're used to. This model allows a small school to create a new learning culture and vision from the beginning,

Table 3.7 Phase In by Grades

Year 0	Year 1	Year 2	Year 3	Year 4
Grades 9–12, 900 students	3 new small schools with 9th-grade students, 75 students in each one	3 new small schools with 150 9th- and 10th-grade students in each one	3 new small schools with 225 9th- through 11th-grade students in each one	3 small schools with 300 students each
	675 10th- through 12th-grade students in large school	450 11th- and 12th-grade students in large school	225 12th-grade students in large school	

with students and faculty buying into it. It also allows a small school to experiment with its practices and structures (e.g., schedule) to find the most effective ones while working with fewer students. Students accustomed to the large school would not be required to change in midcourse.

Challenges: Since the total conversion takes place over a period of four years, it takes longer for all students to be enrolled in a small school. Faculty and students in the large school and those in the small schools might encounter tensions.

Implementation Option 4: Phase Out and Start New Small Schools

With this option, the emerging small schools are intentionally housed in separate facilities until the enrollment empties out of the large school as students graduate; at that time, the emerging small schools are moved back into the facility. This implementation option is often called "hothousing," because the new small schools are housed off-site or in vacant wings of the existing site. As the existing school building empties, it is renovated to later accommodate the new small schools.

> **Example:** A 1,200-student high school redesigns itself into four 300-student small schools. In the first year of implementation, the incoming ninth graders attend a small school in another location. By year four, all of the students from the phased-out school have graduated, and the new small schools move into the facility.

Table 3.8   Phase Out and Start New Schools

Year 0	Year 1	Year 2	Year 3	Year 4
Grades 9–12, 1,200 students	Grade 9 "hothoused" in four new small schools	Grades 9 and 10 "hot-housed" in four new small schools	Grades 9–11 "hothoused" in four new small schools	4 new small schools, each with 300 students in grades 9–12, move into the now vacant facility
	Grades 10–12 remain in existing school	Grades 11 and 12 remain in existing school	Grade 12 remains in existing school	

Advantages: The "phase out and start new" option tends to be successful because it most closely resembles the process of starting freestanding new schools. It avoids the challenge of guiding an existing faculty and staff through a radical change process, because teachers from the old school are usually given the option of joining the new small schools or finding other jobs in the district as the old school is phased out. This option allows the new small schools to be launched unimpeded by the large school culture. It also provides greater freedom to experiment with scheduling, staffing patterns, the curriculum, etc.

Challenges: There may not be facilities available to make this process possible. Many districts do not have the physical space available to hothouse new schools off-site.

CHERRY LANE HIGH CASE STUDY: RESTRUCTURING A LARGE, COMPREHENSIVE HIGH SCHOOL

Lakeview Context

Cherry Lane High School is located in Lakeview,[2] a New England city of 170,000 residents, who are 77% Caucasian, 15% Latino/a, 7% Black, and 5% Asian. The Lakeview Public Schools (LPS) serve 25,500 students, who are 54% Caucasian, 28% Latino/a, 10% Black, and 8% Asian. Fifty-four percent of students are eligible for free/reduced lunch. The school was built in the late 1970s, and many of the school's administrators have worked in the school building since it opened.

All Lakeview secondary schools have been mandated by the district to convert to small learning communities in the next five years. Cherry Lane High began a multiyear effort to convert from a large, comprehensive high school into three small learning communities with unique identities. While the case study documents the school's steps towards improvement, it also highlights the problems inherent in the small learning communities model. Autonomous small schools have greater capacity to improve teaching and learning.

Design Year

A Design Team was formed in September 2001, composed of administrators and teacher volunteers. Faculty committees were also created for governance, staffing, budget, schedule, facilities, and curriculum/assessment. Teachers were compensated for their time. About thirty-five to forty teachers were involved in these smaller planning teams.

The themes of the three small learning communities were based on the current Pathways at Cherry Lane: Information and Technology, Human Services, and Arts, with each community having an assistant principal assigned to lead it. The SLCs were scheduled to roll out gradually, one per year and grade by grade. In this way, the whole school would be converted by school year 2007–08.

The First Small Learning Community Opens at Cherry Lane (2002–2003)

The first small learning community in Cherry Lane High was the Information Technology Academy (ITA), opened in September 2002, with 100 ninth graders and nine faculty. The mission of ITA reads as follows:

> *The Information Technology Academy is a personalized learning environment where students achieve their highest level of success in core academics through a variety of technologies. This academy challenges students and fosters interactive learning experiences. The students are confident, independent, reflective learners who are involved members of the community. Our self-governing faculty is committed to innovative instructional practices. The active participation and support of each student's family is critical to student success and indispensable to the educational process.*

The school day that first year consisted of two main instructional blocks—a three-hour block in the morning and a two-hour block in the afternoon. Teachers had 180 minutes/week of common planning time and approximately 90 minutes per week of individual prep time.

ITA was led by an academic dean, who is also one of the assistant principals. The dean runs ITA in collaboration with a governing board composed of fifteen members: students, the teachers, parents, and community partners from Lakeview Education Partnership.

The faculty committee developed the following guiding practices for use in development of curriculum and assessment.

- Integration of technology throughout the curriculum
- Rigorous and equitable course selections in English, math, science, social studies, foreign language, and technology
- Project-based learning and direct instruction
- Multiple assessments, including a competency checklist and exhibitions
- Graduation requirements include demonstration of mastery over the school's competencies
- State frameworks met through the curriculum design
- Special education services provided to adapt the curriculum to students' needs

Successes

As a result of the conversion to small learning communities, students, teachers, and administrators point to new practices as resulting in tangible changes.

Advisories

Advisories meet every other day for 45 minutes. Students work on goal setting, portfolios, career exploration, reading, and discussions of current events.

> I know how they're doing in every class, if something happens. For some of them it's a good feeling, to know that someone knows how you're doing all around, not just when you're in their classroom. —Teacher

Because teacher teams meet every other day, they can check in with each other on how their advisees are doing in their classes. With a small number of advisees, it is easier to keep track of how students are doing and follow up with parents and teachers if necessary.

> One of the most important things is personalization, so every student is known by a teacher; not just specifically in that discipline, but in all areas of their academics and their life outside of school. . . . It opens communication, helps student achievement. —Teacher

Buy-in for advisories, however, is not complete across ITA staff. Implementation of advisories varies by teacher. However, even the teachers who are uncomfortable serving as advisors see value in advisories.

> Our teachers who are coming to advisory a little reticently but doing it realize that once the kids trust them and know them, the kids react differently to them. . . . They'll do anything for someone they think likes them. —Administrator

Heterogeneous Grouping

ITA is the only academy at Cherry Lane whose design team and staff chose heterogeneous grouping for core academic classes. ITA students are currently divided into four groups representing the full range of prior academic achievement. Special education students are included and receive support from the academy's two inclusion specialists. Each group stays together all day.

> You can't tell me that a student who was expected to function at a low end sitting there participating at some level at a high end isn't gaining something. —Teacher

> The kids see that there is value in one class related to another. . . . Kids are now seeing how it relates to another particular subject. . . . They learn more and they have a variety of ways of improving their academics. —Teacher

> Layered curriculum allows you to make the personalization into an actual piece of work, something that they can do. . . . The kids aren't allowed to stay at a certain level. Once they get better at one level, they're expected to move on. —Teacher

Teacher Change

The smallness of the school allows scheduling for teachers of each grade level to meet regularly. In addition, all students in that grade have the same teachers and all teachers have the same students.

> I'm with a group of teachers that are very helpful, that are committed to what they're doing. And I'm never alone in what I do, you know? We're constantly communicating . . . about everything and anything. —Teacher

> There were a lot of kids in ITA that if they were in the regular population or some-where else, they probably would have never made it through the school year. I think it has to do with the group of teachers that were willing to work together and dis-agree, but come to an agreement, you know? . . . The kid might not be the greatest kid for myself. Teachers took time to say, "Well, this is what he's doing in my class, why don't you try this? He seems to react better to me. Is there a way that we could do something?" —Teacher

Personalization

Because of the smallness of the school, the teaming of teachers, and the implementation of advisories, most students were known and noticed when they were in any kind of trouble, aca-demically or socially. Because they are known well by at least one adult and because their teachers share the same students, students know that teachers are talking about them and caring about them.

> Teachers care; they try their best to help you. . . . They don't want us to fail. —Student

> The closer the relationship you have with the teacher, the more it makes you want to learn, makes you more interested in the class. —Student

Obstacles

Despite the increased collaboration and increased personalization, ITA and Cherry Lane as a whole face a number of obstacles to reaching their initial goal of creating small learning communities.

Budget Cuts

The conversion is occurring during difficult economic times. Districts across the state have expe-rienced drastic budget cuts. Class sizes went from less than 20 in ITA's first year to 28–30.

> It's excruciatingly painful that this took place in an economic downswing… to look across here and see in a 13-by-13 room, thirty kids and me. —Teacher

Budget cuts also affected the ability of the school to increase its capacity to use technol-ogy in all classes.

> We're a technology academy, and students really keep saying, "Where's the technol-ogy?" And I keep saying, "I'm right with you. Where is the technology?" . . . We have lackluster technology. We're not meeting our namesake. —Teacher

Lack of Administrator Autonomy

The budget as it stands does not allow for the small learning communities to have dedicated administrators yet. The academy leaders still have large school responsibilities as assistant principals, making it practically impossible for them to enforce and follow through on all the decisions that each academy has come up with—for example, discipline. While the teachers want some back-up from the administrator on discipline issues, the administrator is too busy fulfilling large school duties to do so.

Buy-In for Rollout

All faculty were forced into a small learning community as of 2004–05. Teachers did not have a choice of going to another district school because the district mandated that all high schools move towards small learning communities.

> They're going to dilute the population of well-meaning, well-intentioned teachers. Everyone who wants to be in a small school is in a small school. And anyone who's not in a small school now doesn't want to be. —Teacher

Many of those faculty who did not want to move to a small learning community described a lack of vision and communication. The assistant principals/deans had too much on their plates to communicate, and too little training in the restructuring effort, to take that task on. As such, staff were ill-informed or misinformed about the changes in their school.

> The communication of a real vision is lacking. —Teacher

> I don't think anyone's done a very good job explaining the rationale of it. —Teacher

Implications for Other Conversion Schools

While each school and district context differs in details, this case study reveals implications with broad relevance to other conversion efforts.

Building Staff Buy-In for the Conversion and Rollout Plan

While the majority of faculty enthusiastically participated in the planning and design for the conversion of Cherry Lane High, they also discussed resistance among a significant number of teachers to a district-mandated initiative. Teachers are skeptical that they will be given decision-making power, that the reform will be sustainable, or that student achievement will improve. A challenge in the coming years is organizing teachers to become empowered in shaping how the small schools will look and feel. This is difficult in a historically administrator-driven culture.

> This is a very veteran staff, and they've seen changes come, and seen changes go. They don't see anything tremendous about this new proposal compared to ten years ago's proposal, twenty years ago's proposal. —Teacher

The Timeline for Rollout

Some teachers felt that the large school would have made more progress if the entire school was required to convert to small learning communities at once.

> Plan the whole building at once. I think everybody would be in the same boat. Everybody would see the successes, and everybody would feel the challenges. Even if the first school is successful, that is not indicative of future success, because that is a special group of teachers who volunteered. If everyone has to volunteer, it's not so frightening. People are concerned and nervous. —Teacher

In the end, Cherry Lane did decide to speed up the rollout of the small learning communities. In 2004–05, the whole school was divided into small learning communities.

Equity Concerns

As Cherry Lane High moves to small learning communities, two student groups have significantly different experiences from the majority of the students at Cherry Lane. The Scholars program is for students identified as gifted in math and science in the seventh grade. Scholars students take all core academic subjects with each other, while only taking electives like health, gym, and music with the general student population. Also, Cherry Lane High is the only district high school physically equipped to serve severely handicapped students; this group of students is housed in its own space on the first floor of the building.

Decision Makers at All Levels Must Communicate Regularly

In the LPS district, the decision for all secondary schools to restructure came from the central office. Yet the messages from the district to the high schools that are converting to small learning communities have not always been consistent; often the central office messages have diverged as they receive new requirements from major funders. Without clarity, those not in decision-making roles lose trust and focus.

> You have to be given the givens. Don't promise us complete autonomy and flexibility in design when we don't have it. Tell us, "this is what you gotta do." This staff was told that we would have complete freedom. —Teacher

All stakeholders, including students, parents, and teachers, must be informed about impending changes that affect their schools. School administrators and Design Teams must have clear goals and means of disseminating information and decisions made at planning meetings. This information should be shared in as many modes as possible—in minutes, memos, and orally at faculty meetings.

SOURCE: Originally published as *Cherry Lane High Case Study: Restructuring a Large, Comprehensive High School to Small Schools* (2003). Boston: Center for Collaborative Education.

TOOLS AND RESOURCES FOR CONVERSIONS

Tool 3.1: Options for Conversion

Purpose: To discuss the options for converting a large school into three smaller schools.

Directions

1. **Present the conversion challenge:** A 1,200-student high school has the goal of eventually creating three small schools within the existing large school facility.

2. **Review the conversion options from Chapter 2:** Redesign All at Once; Phase In by Schools; Phase In by Grades; and Phase Out and Start New.

3. **Small-group discussion:** Break into small groups, examine the options, and discuss which makes the most sense.

4. **Small-group presentation:** Each group presents the model they would choose and the rationale for their choice. Chart reasons.

5. **Large-group discussion:** Facilitate a large-group discussion regarding the advantages and challenges for each option.

Tool 3.2: Strategizing About Barriers to Conversions

Purpose: To better understand the barriers to conversions, and to strategize how to counteract barriers to move the conversion process forward.

Directions

1. **Brainstorm and chart barriers:** Have participants brainstorm all of the potential barriers—including those they may already be experiencing—to converting a large, comprehensive school to small, autonomous schools. These are charted up on the wall. After brainstorming, participants should agree on broad categories under which the barriers could be grouped (e.g., design, capacity, and ownership).

2. **Small-group discussion:** Participants then select a barriers category to work with in small groups. Each group should select ONE prominent barrier within their category and discuss it using the following guiding questions:
   • What are the helping forces counteracting this barrier?
   • What existing resources would you marshal to address this barrier?
   • What strategies would you develop to overcome this barrier?

3. **Large-group discussion:** In a large group, have small groups post and share their responses, using either a gallery walk or a report-out. The large group discusses the main themes, including the commonalities and differences each group displayed in addressing barriers.

Tool 3.3: Common Conversion Design Issues

Purpose: To help participants tackle the most common conversion design issues.

Directions

- **Common Conversion Questions:** Hand out Resource 3.1, "Common Conversion Questions." Post the following five topics:

  1. Faculty and student enrollment

  2. Special groups of students—for example, special education, English language learners, students below grade level, students above grade level

  3. What's big versus what's small—for example, athletics, Advanced Placement courses, electives

  4. The identity of small schools—for example, career themes versus philosophy-based identities

  5. Building community awareness of and support for small schools

- **Select a topic and discuss:** Each participant should select one topic to discuss based on interest and need, with small groups formed by topic. Discuss the topic, using the following guiding three questions:

  1. How is your school currently thinking about this topic?

  2. What are your concerns? What challenges do you face?

  3. How do you think your school should be addressing this topic?

- **Large-group discussion:** Large-group debrief.

Resource 3.1: Common Conversion Questions

In our field experience and research, several common questions raised by staff in large schools converting to small schools sharing a facility have surfaced. It is important to note that every choice has a trade-off, and the path that best meets the small schools' needs should be the one selected.

1. *Which comes first—changing large school structures, culture, or instruction?*

In planning small schools for equity, Design Teams must balance structural, cultural, and instructional change. This is not a linear process; one does not come before the other. Rather, these elements need to occur simultaneously. No one of these three elements alone produces a successful, vibrant, and personalized small school. For example, if small school structures are not used to foster cultural and instructional change, they will not produce changes in student learning. Small school structures are a means to the end goal of creating profound cultural change that results in more personalized relationships between teachers and students, more engaging curriculum and learning experiences for students, and more meaningful assessments of what students have learned. At the same time, instructional changes without structures that enable longer blocks of learning time for students and without a culture in which teachers are committed to engage in discourse about their instructional practice will result in only isolated pockets of teachers who are engaged in innovative instructional practice.

Structures of Small Schools

- Governance structure (e.g., Leadership Teams, governance boards)
- Grouping students and teachers for learning (e.g., smaller learning communities, interdisciplinary teams, heterogeneous grouping and inclusion, looping, multigrade grouping)
- Staffing patterns
- Schedule (e.g., longer blocks of learning, common planning time for faculty)
- Faculty and student assignment
- Student support models (e.g., advisories)

Cultural Change for Small Schools

- Vision building
- Shared and collaborative decision making

- Creating a professional collaborative culture in which faculty are engaged in discourse on their instructional practice and student learning (e.g., Critical Friends Groups)
- Establishing a focus on equity and data (e.g., using multiple sources of student engagement and performance data, creating faculty study groups using a data-based inquiry process to develop solutions for key equity dilemmas)
- Embracing a commitment to student voice and personalization
- Reconceptualizing parent and community engagement (i.e., as partners in the school—through student-parent-teacher conferences, through exhibitions and portfolio reviews, by embedding community in the curriculum)

Instructional Change for Small Schools

- Creating schoolwide habits of mind, or ways of thinking, that are embedded across the curriculum
- Developing schoolwide competencies that all students are expected to demonstrate mastery over in order to graduate, and a curriculum that, through backwards planning, ensures that students meet the school's competencies
- Devising a curriculum to which all students have equitable access, that is focused on the principles of "less is more" and depth over breadth, and that is framed around essential questions and themes
- Framing instruction around the principle of "student-as-worker, teacher-as-coach," with project-based instruction, research projects, and a focus on inquiry
- Differentiating instruction to meet the needs of diverse learners in each classroom
- Building an assessment system in which students must demonstrate mastery over competencies through portfolio reviews, demonstrations, and exhibitions
- Embedding literacy and numeracy throughout the curriculum, using a workshop model

2. *What process should be used to start the conversion conversation among faculty?*

Any process of engaging faculty in conversation about large school conversion should be both top-down and bottom-up. It is clearly helpful to receive a message from the superintendent of a district and the principal that sets forth the rationale and vision of small, personalized, equitable schools. Simultaneously, faculty must be engaged in meaningful conversations about how small schools are a strategy to equity and high achievement. This dialogue should include conversations about using data to understand student engagement and achievement, reading about successful small schools and viewing them firsthand, and participating in the design and the implementation process of the small schools. In this process, the principal may set the parameters for where the school is headed (e.g., "We are going to evolve to become small schools") and then provide ample opportunities for input on how to get there. This process speaks to having Design Teams for each small school and an overarching, representative Leadership Team to guide the schoolwide process of research and design. Schools should begin the cultural change process during the planning process, rather than waiting until the small schools are established. Cultural changes require ample opportunities for team building and professional development in forums such as Critical Friends Groups.

Faculty must have enough time to debate the merits of small schools; however, the process should not be so long that it gets discouraging or enables faculty to become complacent about the structural and cultural changes that need to take place.

3. What should be the identity of the small schools?

Following are two different approaches to conceptualizing the identities of small schools:

- Career themes (for example, health, business, technology, arts)

Advantages: Students will be drawn to and engage in a career theme. Also, career themes attract community partnerships, leading to expanded curriculum opportunities, internships, etc.

Disadvantages: Career themes could lead to tracking by race and income among small schools. Some students may not be ready to think about a career. Also, a career focus could limit students' exposure to broader opportunities.

- Philosophical themes (for example, project-based learning, leadership, social justice)

Advantages: Students can choose a small school in which they can identify with the instructional and philosophical approach. Such schools provide students with a broader educational focus.

Disadvantage: The differences among the small schools may be indistinguishable to some students.

4. What are some options for rolling out new small schools within a large facility?

There are multiple options. All of the factors discussed below are interrelated and mark various points on the spectrum of options.

How are the identities, faculty, and students of new small schools established?

"Big bang" model—A district or principal decides to close a large school down and reopen it as small schools. Teachers and students are assigned equitably to each small school. In the first year, each small school would look essentially the same in schedule, curriculum, student grouping, etc. The identity of each small school would then evolve over subsequent years.

Advantages: This process of creating the new small schools is quick (certainly the prior year could be used as a planning year). It can ensure equity in staff and student assignment. There would be minimal loss of current staffing positions, since the staffing patterns could remain relatively stable the first year.

Disadvantages: The process could result in little buy-in or ownership on the part of both faculty and students. Initially, the small schools would not have unique visions or identities. Each small school could be a replication of the ineffective large school and its practices. This process provides few means to honor existing staff or student relationships. Students would have little to no choice in small school selection.

Design Team model—A request for proposals results in Design Teams of faculty and parents being formed to propose concepts for new small schools within the facility.

Advantages: This model enhances the potential of creating small schools with a strong identity. Design Teams would have high teacher buy-in and sense of ownership. Students would choose a small school based on a commitment to a philosophy or theme.

Disadvantages: This process takes more time than the "big bang" model. It also has the potential to result in imbalances in faculty selection and student enrollment unless there are strong sorting checks in place.

How many schools at a time?

Option 1: One small school the first year, followed by all others the second year

Advantages: The first small school encounters some glitches, so the other schools have the advantage of being able to learn from its experience. Faculty more reluctant or resistant to the small schools reform have time to observe and learn. The entire faculty could benefit from a vision of what the small schools could look like.

Disadvantages: Faculty and student enrollment in the later small schools could be out of balance due to buy-in, with the most enthusiastic faculty and students opting for the first small school. In the first year, faculty in the first small school and those remaining in the large school could feel adversarial or competitive.

Option 2: All small schools the first year

Advantages: The conversion has the same impact across the faculty and student population. It allows for implementation of crossover programs, courses, and services, as well as an evolutionary process from small learning communities to small schools (i.e., there could be many shared services the first year, phased out over time).

Disadvantages: Any significant faculty resistance could impede the conversion. There would be no models of effective small schools already within the facility to learn from.

How many grades at a time?

Option 1: One grade at a time

Advantages: This model allows a small school to create a new learning culture and vision from the beginning, with both students and faculty buying into it. It also allows a small school to experiment with its practices and structures (e.g., schedule) to find the most effective ones while working with fewer students. Students accustomed to the large school would not be required to change in midcourse.

Disadvantages: It takes longer for all students to be enrolled in a small school. Faculty and students in the large school and those in the small schools might encounter tensions.

Option 2: All grades at once

Advantages: The transformation occurs quickly, eliminating the cultural tensions that might occur between students and faculty in the large school and those in the emerging small schools.

Disadvantages: It is likely that it would be a difficult adjustment for upper-grade students, who have been used to being in a large school culture, making it difficult to establish a unique culture and community identity.

Where should new small schools develop?

Hothousing—The emerging small schools are intentionally housed in separate facilities until the enrollment empties out of the large school as students graduate; at that time, the emerging small schools are moved back into the facility.

Advantages: This process allows the new small schools to be launched unimpeded by the large school culture. It also provides greater freedom to experiment with scheduling, staffing patterns, the curriculum, etc.

Disadvantages: There may not be off-site facilities available for this process to occur. Moving new small schools back into the facility is costly.

Using the existing building—Small schools roll out in newly carved-out space in the existing building.

Advantages: New facilities do not have to be found. Schools do not have to move after a year or two of operation. In general, the school creates its own staffing patterns based on needs rather than on existing staffing in a large building.

Disadvantages: Schools must build their vision and identity in a building with an already established history and culture. Schools may assume that the bell schedule and staffing patterns and curricula will stay the same, impeding the development of new ideas and potentially replicating the large school feel.

5. *How do you assign existing faculty to small schools?*

There are several ways in which this could occur, with advantages and disadvantages to each method.

The administration assigns all faculty to the small schools, ensuring equity by discipline, race, gender, and experience.

Advantage: This ensures a balanced, equitable staff.

Disadvantage: Some faculty may not feel ownership over their assigned small school because they had no choice in their assignment.

Faculty submit their rank-ordered choices for preferred small schools. The administration assigns faculty, trying to give everyone their first choice, while balancing each small school for discipline, race, gender, and experience.

Advantage: Faculty get limited choice, while ensuring a balanced, equitable staff.

Disadvantage: Faculty who don't receive their first choice may not feel ownership over their assigned small school.

If the small schools are on a **rollout plan** (one small school each year over several years), the first small school faculty is chosen for the first year, the second small school faculty is chosen the next year, and so forth until all the small schools have been rolled out.

Advantage: The faculty who want to work in each small school, and thus who will have the best chance for making the small school successful, choose to work in one.

Disadvantage: Those most committed to the small schools concept elect to work in the first and second small schools, leaving the more resistant staff for the last small schools.

For the most part, the first two choices have more advantages than the third.

6. How do you assign students to small schools?

Again, there are several ways in which this could occur, with advantages and disadvantages to each method.

Incoming and current students are **assigned by the administration** in order to ensure equitable enrollments by race, gender, income, and achievement level.

Advantage: Each small school has an equitable enrollment, eliminating possibilities of tracking and leveling of the small schools.

Disadvantage: Some students and families may be upset because they do not have a choice.

Incoming and current students have total choice by **lottery,** on a space-available basis.

Advantage: Students get choice in the small school in which they enroll, guaranteeing greater buy-in and more students and families who are committed to the small school's philosophy.

Disadvantage: There is great potential for inequitable enrollments to be created by race, gender, income, and achievement level among the small schools.

Incoming and current students can choose which small school they want to enroll in using a strict, **controlled choice plan** to ensure there is equitable enrollment by race, gender, income, and achievement level among the small schools.

Advantage: Students have some choice, and equitable enrollments among the small schools are also ensured.

Disadvantage: Choice is much more limited in this model, leading to some unhappy students.

Some schools have chosen to start off with strict assignment to ensure equitable enrollments while the identity of the small schools evolve, and after several years, they transition to a controlled choice plan.

7. *What becomes part of the small school, and what remains in the large school?*

The goal of large school conversions is to have as much as possible be embedded in the small schools, so that they can each evolve a unique identity and a personalized learning community among faculty, students, and parents. At the same time, because of economies of scale and a desire to preserve a larger school identity, some activities may remain part of the large school. In considering the right balance between large school and small school, it is helpful to consider the pros and cons of sharing courses and services among small schools housed in one facility.

Having completely autonomous and separate small schools

Advantages: The new small school is better able to develop its own unique identity and community for both faculty and students. The new small school has more control over its resources and practices, such as its schedule.

Disadvantage: There will be fewer offerings of courses and services within each small school.

Sharing courses, programs, and services

Advantages: Students have access to a greater variety of courses, programs, and services, including those courses that would have too few students to warrant a section in a small school (e.g., Advanced Placement Physics).

Disadvantages: The school's identity, sense of community, and degree of personalization can be diluted. Adult accountability is reduced, since students and faculty do not fully identify with one small school.

In many conversion schools, the process of moving to separate, autonomous small schools is a process that takes place over several years in an intentional way, phasing out shared programs, courses, and services to a limited, essential few. Reducing shared courses, in particular, has implications for access to both Advanced Placement (AP) courses and electives. Small schools have several opportunities for both creating access and increasing equity: (1) recruit more students into these courses so that a small school is able to have its own course section in these areas; (2) streamline the number of AP and elective courses offered, making the tough decisions as to the few AP courses and advanced electives that will be the signature of the small school, while eliminating the others; (3) create higher education partnerships in which students can take college courses in subjects that are not offered at the school.

In general, the components that should become part of each small school include the following:

Philosophy and vision

Leadership and governance

Budget

Staffing

Schedule (although each small school may adopt the same block schedule in order to allow for shared electives across the small schools)

All core academic courses

Most electives courses, including academic and arts electives

Most Advanced Placement courses (for which enough students can be recruited)

Advisory

Student support

Special education

Bilingual education

Professional development

Curriculum development and sequence

Shared courses and services that may be offered across the small schools include the following:

Advanced electives and Advanced Placement courses (academic and arts) for which the small school cannot recruit a section of its own

Interscholastic athletics

Health services

For science, the goal should be to relocate all science labs to the separate small schools. They may need to be shared during the first years until this can be accomplished.

In the case of any shared courses, services, programs, or parts of the facility, a buildingwide Leadership Team should coordinate related discussions, deciding on what will be shared and what costs will be charged to each small school. In regard to the facility, this Leadership Team coordinates the following facilities of the large school:

Gymnasium

Auditorium

Cafeteria

Library

The Leadership Team should be representative of all of the small schools housed in the facility, with one of the small school principals serving as the overall building coordinator. In some districts, a buildingwide principal is assigned to the facility for the first few years of a conversion to ensure smooth operations until each small school and the building Leadership Team are more established.

8. *How do small schools address the needs of English language learners (ELL)? Special education students? Students at high achievement levels?*

With each of these groups of students, the goal is equity—ensuring that all students have the same access and opportunity for academic success.

Depending on the number of ELL students, this may mean consolidating them into two or three of the small schools in a large facility, instead of every small school. This concentration allows for adequate courses, support, and services. ELL services and staffing are housed in these select small schools, as is the model of bilingual education service delivery. ELL services are provided in as inclusive a manner as possible.

Special education students are integrated into each small school, as are the services and staffing. The model of special education service delivery is decided upon by each small school, with services provided in as inclusive a manner as possible.

Students of varying achievement levels are not segregated; as much as possible, heterogeneous grouping is the goal and the norm, particularly within the core academic courses. Honors options within regular academic courses can replace the historic leveling of courses into honors and regular levels. Advanced Placement courses become open enrollment courses, with vigorous recruitment of underrepresented groups of students into these courses.

9. *How do you build increased parent and community awareness and support of small schools?*

Building increased community awareness and support of small schools is critical. It is also critical to engage the full diversity of community and parents, particularly parents of low-income students and students of color, and to ensure that not just one group of parents has all of the input. Following are some ideas for accomplishing this:

- Host targeted, invitation-only parent forums on the conversion to small schools, ensuring there is balanced representation at each forum and preventing one group from dominating.
- Create multiple forms of communicating with parents and the community (e.g., communication letters written in the languages spoken in the home, newspaper articles and editorials, brochures discussing the advantages of converting to small schools, cable television shows).

- Have community centers, churches, public housing projects, and other community forums host meetings for parents and community members to discuss the transition to small schools.
- Circulate draft conversion plans for feedback from parents and the community.

10. How can the district play a constructive role in supporting conversions?

District support of large high school conversions is essential if these small schools are going to be sustained over time. Without this support, small schools spend much of their time struggling against district requirements that impede their progress—this is especially true in districts in which there are blanket policies that apply to all schools (e.g., rigid promotion policies, mandated curriculum or instructional minutes for specific disciplines). There are a number of critical areas in which districts can support the conversion of large schools to multiple small, autonomous schools as a means to increasing equitable opportunity and access for students:

- Provide the emerging small schools with charter-like autonomy over budgets, staffing, curriculum, governance, and times. Ensure that small schools have their own designated contiguous space within the facility, clearly marked for easy recognition.
- Ideally, each small school should receive the following autonomies:

Autonomies for Small Schools

Budget: Provide small schools with a lump-sum, per-pupil budget, equal to other district schools within the grade span. Each school may spend its money in the manner that provides the best programs and services to students and their families.

Staffing: Grant small schools the freedom to hire and excess their staff in order to create a unified school community. Allow each school to decide on the staffing pattern that creates the best learning environment for students, hire staff who best fit the needs of the school, and excess staff (into the district pool) who do not fulfill the needs of the school.

Curriculum and assessment: Allow small schools to structure their curriculum and assessment practices to best meet students' learning needs.

Governance and policies: Give small schools the freedom to create their own governance structures, with increased decision-making powers over budget approval, principal selection and firing, and programs and policies.

School calendar: Grant small schools the freedom to set different school days and calendar years for both students and faculty in accordance with their principles or school reform model, with the goal of maximizing learning time for students and collaborative planning time for faculty.

- Adopt a small school policy that charts a course toward small high schools. For example, in 2001 the Oakland, California, public schools adopted a district policy favoring small, autonomous schools, declaring that all new schools, whether in new or existing facilities, would be small, in order to promote the advantages that small schools bring to the achievement of low-income students and students of color. The policy has also served to heighten the awareness and support of parents, community, and public officials.
- Conduct a request-for-proposals process to solicit innovative small school design proposals, and then grant the successful teams planning grants, with ample time to plan for start-up implementation of their new small schools.
- Voice regular and consistent public support for the creation of small schools, citing their value in improving engagement and performance for all students.
- Organize structured and facilitated trips to successful small schools in other districts to build increased support for small schools as well as to give ideas for design and district support to key stakeholders.
- Establish a Leadership Team, representing key constituencies in the district, to oversee and coordinate the district's small schools initiative.

NOTES

1. The last year for which data is available are 2004.
2. This case study is written about a real school in a real district; only the school and district names have been changed.

Building Partnerships to Sustain Small Schools

When the teachers on the ninth-grade team explained how they wanted to include parents in the work they did that year, ninth-grader Rick had been skeptical. Both of his parents worked long hours, and his dad often worked a night shift. But now, halfway through the year, he had to admit it was working—and he liked sharing schoolwork at home better than he had expected. For one thing, the teachers kept it simple. Often all he had to do was read something to his folks, or explain how he had solved a math problem.

Once, for English class, he interviewed his dad about what ninth grade had been like for him. Rick had always thought school had been more serious and strict back then, but it turned out he was wrong—his dad thought Rick was learning a lot more. The best thing about his mom and dad knowing so much about his work in school was that there weren't any surprises. His report cards made a lot more sense to everyone. They seemed to be getting better, too.

WHY ENGAGING FAMILIES AND COMMUNITY IS IMPORTANT

One of the most important ways for schools to improve student learning is to increase family and community involvement. No aspect of school reform is so widely acknowledged as necessary—yet remains so untapped and underdeveloped—as school collaboration with families and communities.

AUTHORS' NOTE: Portions of this chapter were previously published in CCE's Turning Points guide *Creating Partnerships, Bridging Worlds: Family and Community Engagement* (2003).

Very often schools go about the business of restructuring without paying close attention to how all their stakeholders relate to the process of reform, to the school, and to each other. While schools and districts continue to learn how to meet the challenges of meaningfully engaging families and communities, the results of thirty years of research strongly confirm that family involvement is a powerful influence on children's achievement in school: children do better in school when their families are involved (Henderson & Berla, 1994).

Benefits of Parent and Family Involvement in Schools

Henderson and Berla (1994) discuss the benefits of parent and family involvement for students, schools, and the parents* themselves.

Benefits for Students, Teachers, and Schools

- Higher student achievement, grades, and test results
- Better attendance
- Fewer placements in special education programs
- More positive attitudes and behavior
- Higher graduation rates
- Greater enrollment in postsecondary education
- Improved teacher morale
- More support from families

Benefits to Parents

- More confidence in the school
- A more welcoming and inclusive school culture
- Higher opinions of parents by teachers, resulting in higher expectations of their children
- Opportunities for parents to continue their own education

NOTE: *The word *parent* refers to custodial and noncustodial, biological, adoptive, step- and foster mothers and fathers; grandparents; relatives; and any other adult who has a significant role in raising and caring for a child.

Engaging families and communities in partnerships improves school programs and culture, increases parents' skills and leadership, helps teachers with their work, and most important helps children succeed in and out of school. Parents learn things about their own and others' children and bring perspectives from their own segment of the community that can help to inform policy decisions. Involving a diverse group of community members in decision making results in school policies and practices that meet children's needs, represent diverse views, and are credible to the broader school community that must adopt them.

When schools seek to educate students, they are, by default, engaging in relationships with their students' families. Families send their children to school with the faith that they will be respected, cared for, held to high expectations, and supported. Too often this trust has been damaged in our communities. Engaging families in schools involves repairing old relationships and building new ones that demonstrate that families are truly valued partners in the education of students. Schools must go farther to recognize, acknowledge, and address cultural, class, and language differences between teachers and administrators on the one hand and students' families on the other. A school will not achieve equity and excellence for all of the students if it does not acknowledge, understand, and include the families of *all* its students in ways that foster partnership.

Fortunately, by design, small schools offer several advantages over larger schools in achieving the positive results of family engagement. Compared to large schools, small schools have fewer educators for families to meet, smaller gatherings for discussion, and less complex hierarchical structures—all potentially contributing to easier access for families. Small schools personalize their relationships with students and their families, and collaborate with family members in a range of ways—from class-based projects to school governance and policymaking. Small schools have the potential to build stable, consistent, and supportive relationships. This work is based on a vision of schools where all participants— educators, administrators, students, families, district personnel, and community members—can meet to forge new ties and to collaborate around a common interest: that each and every student is supported to achieve at the highest level.

A FRAMEWORK FOR FAMILY ENGAGEMENT

The CCE Framework for Family Engagement is adapted from the work of Dr. Joyce Epstein and colleagues at the Center on School, Family, and Community Partnerships at Johns Hopkins University (Epstein et al., 2002). Epstein and her colleagues identified six major types of family involvement in schools. Together these provide a useful framework for analyzing and developing practices and procedures to engage families. The framework moves parent involvement beyond simply helping out with homework or going to holiday concerts to providing opportunities for parents, communities, and schools to work together to improve their schools, families, and communities. Following are the types of involvement identified.

- *Parenting:* Assisting families with child rearing and education support skills and schools with understanding the diversity of families they serve.
- *Communicating:* Developing several methods of two-way communication between home and school.
- *Volunteering:* Creating ways families can be involved in the school and effective methods of recruiting them.
- *Learning:* Linking families with their children's curriculum through learning activities and homework in which families can participate.
- *Collaborative decision making:* Including families as decision makers, advocates, and members of school councils and committees.
- *Collaborating with the community:* Coordinating services in the community with family needs and providing services to the community.

SAMPLE PRACTICES FOR FAMILY AND COMMUNITY INVOLVEMENT

Within each of the six involvement areas described above, there are probably dozens of possible activities. The framework acknowledges that engagement can happen in many ways, with many levels of success. Each school community's goal is to adapt and build upon the framework to fit their local conditions.

Parenting

Families provide for the health and safety of their children, and maintain a home environment that encourages learning and positive behavior in school. Schools can reciprocate by providing training and information to help families understand their children's development and how to support the challenges and developmental changes students face. Staff at effective small schools are committed to understanding students and their families.

Sample parent involvement activities:

- Create a parent center, or place in the school for parents and families, with comfortable furniture, a phone, coffeepot, bulletin board with announcements, and resource materials.
- Offer workshops to parents on school-related and parenting issues, such as making the most of a parent-teacher conference, increasing children's motivation to learn, encouraging reading in the home, conflict prevention, discipline strategies, and understanding the developmental stages and challenges of children and their learning.

Communicating

Effective communication among members of the school, home, and community is a crucial element in the framework for parent and community involvement. Schools need to reach out to families with information about school programs and student progress. All communication should be ongoing, two-way, and presented in a variety of formats. Communication should be easily understood, free of jargon, and in a language spoken by the family at home.

Sample communication activities:

- Make parents and community members feel welcome in the school with prominent welcome signs, friendly staff, orientations/open houses, and "user friendly" school directories and maps.
- Establish ongoing methods of communication that are two-way, such as parent-teacher contracts, notes for keeping in touch, telephone conversations, email, classroom newsletters, and letters from home for parents to provide information to educators about their child.
- Provide a minimum of two conferences per year with parents (and possibly students) to discuss individual student achievement and to establish a plan for progress.

Friendliness at the Front Door

If you want visitors to feel welcome at your school, your school entrance and building need to convey that message loud and clear. Here are some very simple and doable changes you can make to welcome your families and community members from the first minute they walk through the door.

- *Welcome sign:* Put up a sign that says "Welcome" in the languages of your community at the entrance (and even outside if your front door entrance is not clearly visible).
- *Bulletin boards and information tables:* Put out bulletin boards or tables with notices, calendars of events, forms to fill out, deadlines, reminders, news, and other interesting information.
- *Staff poster:* Make a poster with every staff member's photograph, name, subject, and grade level. Post it in the entrance.
- *Clear directions:* Provide large signs directing people to the main office, principal, counselor, and other important offices, and to the different small schools in the building.
- *Maps:* Create several reader-friendly maps of the school and post in several locations. Prominently distinguish the boundaries of each small school in the building.

Volunteering

Schools can welcome and actively seek assistance from parent and community volunteers. Parents and community members share responsibility for students' academic achievement and their personal and social development by making significant contributions to the environment and functions of the school. To enable more parents and community members to participate, schools can create flexible schedules and match the talents and interests of parents and others who want to help out to the needs of students, teachers, and administrators. Volunteers are valued for their efforts in whatever capacity they are able to participate. Even minor participation can provide a basis for future collaboration and involvement.

Sample volunteering activities

- Poll parents and community members about special skills, talents, and experiences they can share with students as part of classroom activities. Set up this information in a volunteer database and distribute to staff for easy access.
- Recognize volunteers' contributions in newsletters, ceremonies, or certificates of appreciation.

Learning

Families and community members, as well as teachers, play an integral role in assisting student learning. With the guidance and support of teachers, family members and community programs can supervise and assist students at home with homework assignments and other school-related activities. With more opportunities to relate and apply school learning to home and community settings, students connect the school curriculum to skills that are required in the real world.

Sample student learning activities

- Engage parents as reviewers of student exhibitions and portfolios.
- Host student-teacher-parent conferences to assess student progress.
- Involve parents in developing the school's curriculum and setting learning goals for students.
- Design homework tasks that require students and families to interact so parents become aware of what and how their children are learning.

"FamTek" at Greater Egleston Community High School, Boston, MA

The recent explosion of the use of information technology has brought about a noticeable gap in many communities between the knowledge, skills, and experiences of young adults and those of their parents and other adults in their communities. High school students at the Greater Egleston High School in Boston discovered that their parents wanted help in closing the computer gap, also known as the "digital divide"—and they were willing to learn these new skills from the students themselves.

As a result, the student-designed and -taught "FamTek" program was born. As part of their community service classes, students design the course content, materials, and instruction for a course they teach in the evenings over a six-week period to parents who sign up. The course has covered everything from the mouse, navigating Windows and word processing to using Excel, PowerPoint, email, and the Web. The project was designed not only to increase parent familiarity with and enjoyment of computers, but also for students to learn some hard lessons about what it means to be a teacher, including making (and sticking to) rules for attendance and requirements for completion, and how to diversify their teaching to meet the needs of the range of learners in a course.

Parents with up to two excused absences are eligible for a "certificate of completion." They must also create a piece of individual work that shows the lesson they've learned, and they are asked to share a portfolio of their work at an "end-of-course celebration." The school has been able to pay students a $10/hour stipend for teaching, and they recommend that students are provided incentives for returning to the school in the evening to teach long after school has ended. Participating family members also receive a new or refurbished computer upon completing the program. After each course is taught, the "teachers" are asked to provide a written report about their experience and to revise their course, if necessary.

After two years of sharing his computer savvy with parents, a senior has completely taken over organizing the program—a community-action project, also known as a CAP—for both students and parents and is looking into teaching as a career.

Collaborative Decision Making

Parents and community members have meaningful roles in the collaborative processes of school planning and decision making. Collaboration with parent and community groups brings additional skills, resources, and points of view to support school improvement. Small schools can realistically survey large portions of their population to gather feedback about changes and can adjust more quickly to changing needs and problems. Parents and community members can be important advocates for improving public education.

Sample collaborative decision-making activities

- Make sure parents and community members are represented on planning and advisory committees and the school council.
- Seek parent and community input on school policies related to budget, teacher and principal hiring, schoolwide plans, and parent involvement.

Collaborating With the Community

Schools can help families gain access to support services such as health care, cultural events, tutoring services, and afterschool child-care programs offered by community organizations and agencies. Schools and students can contribute services to the community. The school itself can become a resource for families and community members by extending its hours of operation and providing its facilities for community meetings, adult education, local theatrical events, health screenings, etc.

Sample community partnership activities

- Engage community groups such as service organizations, churches and religious groups, cultural organizations, social service agencies, and businesses in collaborative efforts to improve student learning and family life.
- Develop partnerships that encourage local businesses, universities, and service providers to help prepare students for the world of work and civic responsibility.

GETTING STARTED: DEVELOPING PLANS FOR FAMILY ENGAGEMENT

As one teacher in a small school commented, "family and community engagement is often at the top of a school's 'To Do List,' but is almost always the last thing addressed." This may be partly because other priorities seem more immediate and partly because the task can seem particularly overwhelming. Often teachers see family and community engagement as "another" activity added to their already full agendas. Teachers need time for learning and developing leadership skills and strategies for effective communication and group facilitation.

Establish a Family Engagement Study Group

One way to tackle time barriers is to establish a committee or study group to focus on family engagement and ensure that all stakeholders in the school are represented (students, parents, teachers, community groups).

Determine early on who will be in the group, how often and when it will meet, and how the group will communicate its work to the schoolwide community. This group's charge will be, first, to assess the school's current practices and climate regarding family-community engagement, perhaps by reviewing Resource 4.1, "Framework of Focus Areas for Involvement and Sample Practices," and to use this assessment to prepare a plan of action for the school community to review and adopt. The group may also oversee implementation of its plan, but membership in the group may expand to include those responsible for carrying out particular aspects of the plan.

Use Data-Based Inquiry for Planning

The family-community engagement group should undertake a formal inquiry process concerning the school and its community. Appropriate avenues for this study group's inquiry include using data from a variety of sources to identify areas of challenge for the school; developing a simple questionnaire to find out what families currently think of the school's climate; analyzing student achievement data; and gathering information about what kinds of organizations (government, nonprofit, commercial, and other) are based in the immediate geographical area. Schools can also begin to find out about the values, skills, and dreams of students and their families; the racial/ethnic, language, and class mix of its community; and changes that have taken place in the community over time. Students can be involved in this process by assisting with research, surveys, other investigation, and reporting. In addition, the family and community engagement group should take part in reading about, doing research on, and visiting model schools and programs.

Create a Vision

Often schools approach the task of engaging families by creating new activities one at a time in a piecemeal fashion, resulting in a hodgepodge of disconnected and overlapping programs that are carried out by different parties. The resulting structure—or lack thereof—often confuses staff and parents alike and can lead to frustration and conflict. One job of the study group is to create a vision and set goals and objectives for community and parent engagement. This vision should provide a coherent framework that can help the school to steer its work.

Reaching All Parents

Some parents consider volunteering at their child's school an integral part of being a parent and derive satisfaction from successful interactions between home and school. Often, simply because it is easy, schools call on these same "activist" parents when volunteers or parent representatives on committees are needed. Many other parents, however, are unable to participate for a variety of reasons. Barriers to these parents' participation include having unsuccessful school experiences in the past themselves, having work schedules that make volunteering difficult, not knowing how to help out, having limited proficiency in English, or coming from cultures where parent involvement in the school life of their children is not the norm. Schools need to make an extra effort to invite participation and broaden the list of parents who represent the school. When schools encourage parent involvement in positive ways, parents usually respond enthusiastically.

TOOLS AND RESOURCES FOR BUILDING PARTNERSHIPS: CREATING SCHOOLS AS CENTERS FOR LEARNING

Tool 4.1: Community Walk

Purpose: To strengthen faculty understanding and knowledge of the community surrounding the school and/or the communities in which students live; to build trust and collaboration among teachers, students, and families; and to lay a foundation for future community partnerships that support curriculum and instruction and student development.

Directions

Participants: Teachers, administrators, students, parents.

Overall Structure of the Day

- An organizing team or committee determines ahead of time who will participate and forms small groups of five or six (ideally a mix of students, teachers, and parents).
- The organizing team should conduct its own preliminary exploration to survey the area and determine what information and resources to provide to participants. You may want to assign each group a different quadrant on the map.
- Provide a set of common resources (map, preliminary list of community organizations, journal, etc.) without overly dictating the flow of the day. You want to allow for individual and group discoveries and surprises.
- Begin the day with a large-group framing activity, and end the day with a sharing of discoveries.
- Collect and document the community resources—people, organizations, places—"discovered" by the small groups.

Sample Activities

- People may be nervous. In the large group in the morning, do a couple of fun, icebreaker activities and a discussion about goals and concerns. (There are many sources of icebreaker activities. The books of games and activities published by Project Adventure are one good source; see list at http://www.pa.org/publications.asp)
- Arrange a certain number of interviews and/or site visits ahead of time, but leave each group with plenty of room to explore.
- Open-ended anchor activities are a good way to structure the day:
  - Stop and interview at least three passersby. Sample questions might be, "What do you know about the school?" "What do you think school students most need?"
  - Give each group of five or six people a limited amount of money for lunch (ask them not to supplement). Ask them to be creative and find lunch for the whole group within their budget.

○ Provide small journals and ask participants to stop several times during the day and reflect on their learning. Sample journal prompts might include
  – What is community?
  – List as many sights, sounds, and smells as you can in five minutes.
  – Conduct an inventory of the buildings on one or two blocks—list all of the buildings and organize them into categories by type or organization (e.g., residences, stores).
  – What are you finding most surprising about this exploration?

At the end of the day, provide each small group with newsprint markers and other art materials and ask them to create a visual "map" of their exploration. Explain that maps can represent more than physical landmarks, and ask them to be creative. A final gallery walk will allow participants to share the results and feelings from the day.

SOURCE: Adapted from Rugen, L. (1995). The one-day community exploration: An expeditionary learning professional development experience. In E. Cousins and M. Rogers (Eds.), *Fieldwork: Vol. 1* (pp. 122–125) Dubuque, IA: Kendall/Hunt. The version presented here originally appeared in CCE's publication *Creating Partnerships, Bridging Worlds: Family and Community Engagement* (2003).

Tool 4.2: Student-Led Conferences

Purpose: To provide guidelines for student-led conferences.

Directions: Use these guidelines for student-led conferences. In a student-led conference, the student is in charge of presenting his or her work and progress to parents. The teacher acts as facilitator.

1. **Preparation:** Be sure to allow ample time to help students prepare for the conference by having them engage in these steps:
   • Gathering and reflecting on examples of their work and evidence of their progress.
   • Learning how to lead the conference, including how to explain and interpret their work and information about what they are learning.
   • Practicing the presentations through role-play.

   Offer clear written guidelines to parents about the purpose and structure of student-led conferences, particularly if it is a new process.

2. **The conference:** Some schools schedule several conferences simultaneously, with the teacher available to answer questions. Others structure them so the teacher will be present for the entire conference, but participate only when necessary.
   • Focus the conference on discussing evidence of learning (through an ongoing portfolio of work or artifacts gathered specifically for the conference) and on goals set for the future. Grades should be a secondary focus.
   • Encourage a balance of intellectual, social, and emotional aspects of learning.
   • Rather than getting stuck on past failures, students and parents should be encouraged to engage in problem solving and goal setting. A written action plan signed by student and parent(s) is often helpful.
   • Allow 20–30 minutes for each conference.

3. **Evaluation:** Allow time at the end of each conference, or soon after, for students, parents, and teachers to reflect on the effectiveness of the conference—both the student-led format and their particular conference. A brief evaluation form can be helpful.

SOURCE: Adapted from Hackmann, D. (1997). *Student-led conferences at the middle level.* Champaign, IL: ERIC Clearinghouse on Elementary and Early Childhood Education. (ERIC Digest No. ED407171)

Tool 4.3: Parent-Teacher Conferences

Purpose: To provide guidelines for productive parent-teacher conferences and conversations.

Directions

Overview: Why are parent-teacher conferences often so tense? If there are difficult issues to be discussed, participants often wind up feeling awkward, strained, or defensive. For parents and caregivers, nothing matters more than the well-being and success of their child. If a child is struggling, parents often take it to heart as their own failure in parenting. For teachers, a child's difficulties or failures are often felt—or taken—as their own failure in teaching. No wonder having an honest, productive conversation is so difficult!

As the facilitators of such conversations, teachers need to prepare for parent-teacher conferences and consider the following guidelines about listening and giving and receiving feedback.

Welcoming and Framing

1. Begin the conference by welcoming the parent(s)/caregiver(s). Review your goals and agenda for the conference. . . . *Ask for their goals.*

Offering Your Perspective on the Student and Giving Feedback

2. Begin with an assessment of the student's strengths and unique positive qualities.

3. Focus your assessment of the student's needs/challenges:
   - Give feedback with care—to be useful, feedback needs to be given in the spirit of wanting to help the student.
   - Be specific—feedback is most useful when it is concrete and refers to specific evidence (events, behaviors, examples of work, etc.).
   - Speak for yourself, and include feelings. Use "I" statements when talking. Discuss only things you have witnessed, not what others may have told you. Personalize your comments and be empathetic.
   - Avoid evaluative labels and judgments. In general, feedback is most useful if it is specific and does not include general labels such as "good," "bad," "irresponsible," "lazy," etc.
   - Focus on what is actionable. Ideally, feedback in a parent-teacher conference should focus on what all parties (parent, student, teacher) can change. Agreeing on concrete follow-up steps is often the best way to close a conference.

Hearing the Parents' Perspective: Listening and Receiving Feedback

4. Ask for parents' or caregivers' assessment of the student. What do they see as the child's unique strengths and needs? What are their concerns? How do they respond to what the teacher presented?

5. If there are strong feelings that are difficult to hear, remember the following guidelines:
   - Breathe—Remembering this simple act can make a difference, helping you relax and focus.

- Listen carefully—Don't interrupt the parent(s), defend, or justify. Give ample time for them to fully explain their thoughts. Indicate with body language (nods, eye contact, etc.) that you are fully present.
- Ask questions to clarify your understanding of the concerns.
- Summarize or paraphrase what you heard in your own words.
- Take time to sort out what you heard. You may need time to think about an issue and get back to the parent, but be sure that you do follow up.

6. Always close a conference with concrete next steps and with an expression of appreciation for parents' time, perspectives, and concerns.

SOURCE: Adapted from Dunne, F. (1996.) *Principles of giving feedback*. Bloomington, IN: National School Reform Faculty.

RESOURCE 4.1: FRAMEWORK OF FOCUS AREAS FOR INVOLVEMENT AND SAMPLE PRACTICES

Focus Area	Parenting	Communicating	Volunteering
Type of Involvement	Assisting families with parenting and child-rearing skills, and schools in understanding families	Developing effective communication from home to school and school to home	Creating ways that families can be involved in the school and effective methods of recruitment
Sample Practices	Make personal contact through parent-teacher conferences, home visits, and parent liaisons. Conduct tours and interviews in the communities in which students live to learn about different cultures, strengths, resources, and needs. Create a parent center with comfortable furniture, phone, coffeepot, bulletin board with announcements, and resource materials. Help parents understand their roles in the school/family/community partnership, such as getting to know the child's teacher, asking questions, participating in school activities, and monitoring homework.	Make parents and community members feel welcome in the school with prominent welcome signs, friendly staff, orientations/open houses, "user friendly" school directories and maps (in the home languages of students). Introduce school policies and programs at the beginning of the year with welcome letters, information packets, school calendars, and information sessions that are manageable and family friendly. Establish ongoing methods of two-way communication, such as parent-teacher contracts, notes for keeping in touch, telephone conversations, email, classroom newsletters, and letters from home for parents to provide information to educators about their child.	Poll parents and community members about their special skills, talents, and experiences so they can share them with students as part of classroom activities. Set up this information in a volunteer database and distribute to staff for easy access. Encourage parents to sign up early in the year for specific activities to help out at the school. Provide volunteers with adequate training. Recognize volunteers' contributions in ways such as newsletters, ceremonies, and certificates of appreciation. Create parent patrols or other activities to aid in safety and in operation of school programs.

Conduct workshops for parents on school and parenting issues, such as how to make the most of a parent-teacher conference, how to increase a child's motivation to learn, and how to encourage reading in the home.

Foster parent involvement through strategies including informal school-family gatherings, workshops, and special events.

Create opportunities for families and community members to visit the school—Open houses, classroom observations, class parties, etc.

Link parents to community resources such as youth organizations, nutrition programs, and counseling agencies.

Develop ways to communicate with parents whose first language is not English, involving staff and school volunteers of diverse backgrounds to make families comfortable.

Use cassette tapes to present information to parents with low literacy skills.

Celebrate student work through various school displays and programs.

Create opportunities for families to participate in classrooms as either experts on topics or teachers' aides.

Enlist family and community members as audience members and evaluators of student performances and exhibitions.

(Continued)

Resource 4.1 (Continued)

Focus Area	Student Learning	Collaborative Decision Making	Collaborating With the Community
Type of Involvement	Linking families with their children's curriculum through learning activities that can be done at home, as well as through homework	Including families as decision makers, advocates, members of schools councils, and committees	Coordinating services in the community with family needs, and providing services to the community
Sample Practices	Share information with families on skills required for students in all subjects at each grade.	Promote active PTA/PTO or other parent organizations, advisory councils, or committees (e.g., curriculum, safety, personnel) for parent leadership and participation.	Provide information for students and families on community health, cultural, recreational, social support, and other programs or services.
	Share information on homework policies and how to monitor and discuss schoolwork at home.		
	Share information on how to assist students to improve skills on various class and school assessments.	Establish independent advocacy groups to lobby and work for school reform and improvements.	Give information on community activities that link to learning skills and talents, including summer programs for students.
	Create a regular schedule of homework that requires students to discuss and interact with families on what they are learning in class.		Promote service integration through partnerships involving schools, businesses, and other agencies and organizations (civic, counseling, cultural, health, recreational).
	Provide calendars with activities for parents and students at home.	Educate parents and community members about the roles and responsibilities of school committees, superintendents, principals, and school councils.	
	Hold family math, science, and reading activities at school.		
	Give out summer learning packets or ideas for activities.		Encourage service to the community by students, families, and schools (e.g., recycling, art, music, drama, and other activities for seniors or others).
	Encourage family participation in setting student goals each year and in planning for college or work.	Encourage parent and community participation at the school, district, state, and national levels to address issues that impact student learning.	
	Establish a mentoring program that involves families, communities, and school participants.		

SOURCES: These processes, actions, activities, and strategies are adapted from a variety of sources, including Ballen and Moles (1994), Bamber, Berla and Henderson (1996), Christenson and Sheridan (2001), Davis (2000), Dianda and McLaren (1996), Epstein et al. (2002), and Funkhouser and Gonzales (1997).

PART II

Learning and Achievement in Each Small School

Teaching, Learning, and Assessment for High Achievement for All Learners

Just like backstage before opening night, the energy in the hallways at East High School at the end-of-the-year Student Exhibition Day is charged with excitement and anticipation. One student is going over his notes and posters, getting ready to discuss a cross-section of African American achievements in several fields. Another student makes sure her PowerPoint presentation explaining how the city will get through another hot summer without power outages is ready to go. A third student stretches before performing an original dance and then discussing how the dance was created within a historical context of dance in America.

In the school lobby, members of the judging panels—faculty, parents, and experts from the community—sip coffee and eat doughnuts while they anxiously wait for the exhibitions to begin. Now in their third year of using final exhibitions as one criterion for graduation, members of the East High School community are proud of this day. Not only does it represent a culminating experience for each individual high school senior, but it is also the result of the school's vision that all students will learn to use their minds well. Well-developed rubrics in hand for grading each student, the assessors are ready to get started.

RETHINKING CURRICULUM, INSTRUCTION, AND ASSESSMENT

Like many small schools, East High School has made a big transition from simply handing out quarterly grades to implementing a system of

---

AUTHOR'S NOTE: Portions of this chapter were previously published in CCE's Turning Points guides: *Turning Points Guide to Curriculum Development* (2001), *Teaching Literacy in the Turning Points School* (2001), and *Understanding Learning: Assessment in the Turning Points School* (2005).

assessment that includes portfolios, exhibitions, performances, and celebrations. All forms of assessment are deeply embedded in the curriculum and involve a student presenting an aspect of academic work in order to exhibit mastery of content and skills. Rubrics are designed to guide the assessment and carefully spell out how to assess if a student is using the school's habits of mind and can demonstrate content mastery. This move to assessment by exhibition is a result of a thorough reexamination of what the school thinks students should know and be able to do. It has also led to a reexamination of the curriculum and instruction that will prepare all students to succeed in meeting the school's competencies. Teachers cannot assess students' abilities to use knowledge and skills unless they give them important work to do. Effective instruction offers students the support and guidance they need to tackle such important work. When students are engaged and interested in a task, they are more likely to do their best work.

Traditionally, a school's curriculum has been viewed as a vast body of knowledge divided into several subject areas (math, social studies, English, the sciences, languages, etc.) that students are asked to "cover" and learn in a given period of time. In this race to cover material, learning often becomes a question of memorizing or accumulating facts and information that are quickly forgotten once students leave school. Cognitive theorists in the last few decades have established that simply memorizing or accumulating facts does not mean that humans are engaged in learning. Learning is an active process: a student learns through experience, by thinking (using his/her mind well), acquiring information in a meaningful context, and applying it to new situations or problems.

This notion of learning as an active process has implications for how small schools develop curricula. Instead of trying to cover a broad range of content, effective small schools find ways to limit and simplify what students learn. Schools redesign their curricular offerings with a focus on teaching students to think, develop habits of mind, and become competent in those areas that are most important.

When members of the High School Restructuring Task Force sat down with focus groups of students and teachers at different city high schools, they witnessed the challenge and complexity of "achieving high standards." Students spoke about what it meant to be challenged academically and to feel as though they were really learning. Almost every student had experienced a teacher or class that had pushed him/her to think. The stories were very specific— an essay in history that required students to imagine living in a different historical period, a long-term research project, a very "intense" teacher who gave homework every night. When the conversation shifted to what the students felt needed to change, they said that such challenging classes were rare. Much of the time they were not asked to do very much except take notes or copy things from the board. They were rarely given homework. They did not have many books. Often they were so bored they either slept through class or acted up.

The teachers in the focus groups had a very different perspective from the students. They felt that, despite their best efforts, a small group of very disruptive students made it close to impossible to teach well. Many of their students came to high school unprepared—without the skills to do high school math and reading well below grade level. Some teachers wondered whether raising the standards for graduation would result only in a higher dropout rate. Students were not meeting minimum standards of competency now—how would they "achieve high standards"?

To some teachers, it seemed counterintuitive to raise standards and create a challenging curriculum for all students when one has not seen evidence of students' abilities to meet them, and yet, they believed, that is what must happen for any significant improvement in learning to occur. As the students in the focus groups demonstrated, respect and engagement stem from real challenge: they are not prerequisites. Other school restructuring practices must be in place to support and create the conditions for powerful learning, but the starting and ending point of every plan and every conversation needs to be what happens between and among teachers and students.

—Boston Public Schools/Boston Teachers Union
High School Restructuring Task Force, 1998, p. 20

A FRAMEWORK FOR CURRICULUM, INSTRUCTION, AND ASSESSMENT: WHAT DO WE WANT ALL STUDENTS TO KNOW AND BE ABLE TO DO?

The central goal of all schools should be to teach all students to "use their minds well in every area of work they undertake." Schools should strive to engage each student in a meaningful curriculum that has applications in the real world. These goals have implications for how schools develop curricula, what instructional practices they use, and how they assess their students.

The four principles described below provide a framework to guide curriculum development, instruction, and assessment in small schools.

1. *Overarching Vision for Teaching and Learning*
   o Habits of Mind: The school's central goal is to teach children to use their minds well in every area of work they undertake, with the result that they become responsible members of a democratic community.

2. *Curriculum*
   • Less Is More: The school's curriculum is driven by the concept of "less is more." Each student should master a limited number of essential skills and understandings.

3. *Instruction*
   • Student-as-Worker; Teacher-as-Coach: The governing metaphor of the school should be student-as-worker and teacher-as-coach. This helps students to take responsibility for their learning. Learning should be purposeful, rigorous, and related to helping students become powerful in the real world.

4. *Assessment*
   • Assessment by Exhibition: Assessment should demonstrate what important things students know and can do, as well as where they are in need of more help. Students should demonstrate their mastery of competencies in various ways, including through exhibitions and portfolios. They should learn to assess their own learning and work and be given regular opportunities to reflect.

HABITS OF MIND: DEFINING AN OVERARCHING VISION FOR TEACHING AND LEARNING

Small schools help students acquire and develop habits of mind. Developed over time, a habit is a pattern of behavior that occurs without thought on the part of the individual. Students acquire habits of mind that assist learning through frequent repetition of specific patterns of thinking and ways of looking at the world. Making suppositions, asking questions, reasoning, making connections, looking for evidence, and recognizing perspectives are all considered habits of mind. A school's habits of mind should guide every aspect of its organization and its approach to teaching and learning. They present a vision of the kind of learner and the kind of community member we want every student to become.

Habits of mind are the lenses through which students see, figure out, and appreciate their world. They guide students' thinking, actions, and interactions. For example, when a student considers the documentation of a historical event, one habit of mind might be to use multiple perspectives and ask, *Whose viewpoint is represented here?* If students were to conduct field research at a national park, they would look for evidence of past inhabitants. If students are engaged in a controversy over a school rule—say, something as mundane as "no hats in class"—they should be asked to consider and discuss the multiple viewpoints on the issue.

Habits of mind cross all content areas. Students may be asked to look for patterns in mathematics, but they also use this habit of mind in their study of world literature, their personal behavior, and the sciences.

Habits of mind are connected to *dispositions*—the feelings, attitudes, values, and interests possessed by the learner. This is a complex area that goes beyond the intellect to areas of personal development and emotion. Often teachers set broad goals to the effect that students will become "self-directed learners" or "develop a love of reading." These goals acknowledge the importance of the emotional domain to student learning. Some schools distinguish between habits of *mind* and habits of *heart* or work to make explicit the social/emotional domain.

Teaching students to use their minds well in every area of work they undertake is the central goal of small schools. All instructional practices, curriculum development, and assessment experiences are guided by the question, *What ways of thinking and acting do we want our students to develop and acquire?*

The Habits of Mind of the Mission Hill School, Boston, MA

The Mission Hill Habits of Mind are an approach to both the traditional academic disciplines (math, science, literature, and history) and the interdisciplinary stuff of ordinary life. They are what lead us to ask good questions and seek solid answers. They are our definition of a well-educated person.

Evidence: How do we know what's true and false? What evidence counts? How sure can we be? What makes it credible to us? This includes using the scientific method and more.

Viewpoint: How else might this look if we stepped into other shoes? If we were looking at it from a different direction? If we had a different history or expectations? This requires the exercise of informed "empathy" and imagination. It requires flexibility of mind.

Connections/Cause and Effect: Is there a pattern? Have we seen something like this before? What are the possible consequences?

Conjecture: Could it have been otherwise? Supposing that? What if? This habit requires use of imagination as well as knowledge of alternative possibilities. It includes the habits described above.

Relevance: Does it matter? Who cares?

None of these five habits stands separately. And the ways we use such habits differ, depending on whether we are studying a mathematical proof, a scientific hypothesis, a historical dispute, a debate over economics, the appreciation of a piece of art, a critique of a novel, the telling of a myth or a narrative, or the settling of a playground dispute.

The Mission Hill Habits of Mind are supplemented by *Habits of Work:* the habit of meeting deadlines, being on time, sticking to a task, not getting frustrated quickly, hearing out what others have to say, and more.

Both sets of "habits" are developed in the process of gathering appropriate knowledge and skill in school and out. The best test is whether students use such habits in the course of their work. And again, not just in school. Knowing "how-to" is no substitute for having good habits. Who cares if you could drive well, if you're not in the habit of mind of doing so? Who cares if you could be on time, if you never are?

SOURCE: Used with permission of the Mission Hill School.

LESS IS MORE: AN APPROACH TO CURRICULUM DESIGN

In approaching curriculum, the "less is more" principle asks schools to streamline their learning goals so students can master a limited number of essential skills and areas of knowledge rather than attempting to learn the vast amount of content that is usually included in the traditional subject areas. Instead of racing to cover lots of material within a given unit, semester, or school year, students and teachers design curricula by asking what are the essential skills and areas of knowledge related to the needs and interests of the students. Students learn when they have the time to think things through, and do not end up simply memorizing or accumulating a set of facts. Developing this "depth-over-breadth" curriculum requires schools to make hard decisions: to truly engage students in meaningful intellectual work takes time. Schools have to find ways to decide which electives, for example, can be cut from or integrated within the redesigned curriculum.

During a course of study, students acquire knowledge from different areas while developing skills to understand and use that knowledge in real-life situations. For example, students gain understanding of the causes of the Civil War while developing skills such as gathering evidence from different types of historical sources and making connections to current events they read about in the newspaper.

The curriculum should be based on a set of competencies the school has developed as expectations for graduation (from elementary, middle, or high school). These learning competencies encompass the school's habits of mind, essential understandings, and essential skills. Students and families are introduced to the graduation competencies as they enroll in the school.

Competencies are limited so that the focus is on student learning and not on how much material is covered. From the beginning, learning competencies are shared and often developed with students. If students know what they are striving for, they will be better able to assess their progress along the way. While learning competencies are the same for all students, how students meet them may vary, depending on student interest, learning needs, and achievement level.

STUDENT-AS-WORKER, TEACHER-AS-COACH: AN APPROACH TO INSTRUCTION

Once the learning competencies—habits of mind, knowledge area, and essential skills—for a unit of study have been clearly defined, teachers look for ways to engage students in learning experiences that are purposeful, challenging, and related to helping students become powerful in the real world. This means moving beyond textbook-based instruction toward instruction that incorporates a wide variety of materials and strategies and promotes challenging intellectual work that connects to the real lives of the students.

When students and teachers engage in such active learning, there is a shift in traditional classroom roles. As students become "workers," they assume ownership and greater responsibility for their learning. The "teacher-as-coach" becomes a facilitator of learning, guiding students in discussions, setting up projects, locating resources, and linking students' work with their community.

A critical role of the "teacher-as-coach" is modeling the different skills being taught. Instruction should employ a "gradual release of responsibility" model of teaching (Keene & Zimmerman, 1997) that moves from a teacher's modeling and direct instruction to students' taking responsibility for demonstrating their knowledge and use of particular content and skills. The process is repeated as new content or skills are introduced. In addition to modeling and directly teaching skills and content, teachers need to provide students with ample opportunity to make choices and take responsibility for their learning. There are several basic components of this model of teaching.

- Begin with what students know and their life outside of school—tap students' interests and curiosity.
- Understand where students are starting from, and build skills in a progression to stretch their learning (scaffolding).
- Introduce a new concept, model it, have students practice it while guided by the teacher, practice in small groups or pairs, and then practice independently. Responsibility moves from the teacher to groups of students to the individual.
- Provide examples of high-quality work that students can analyze and emulate.

Teachers look for ways to maximize each student's growth by meeting each student at his or her readiness level and helping students to progress and be challenged. To accommodate the wide range of learners in their classrooms, teachers differentiate instruction and devise a variety of assessments and learning experiences that demonstrates the different elements of student understanding. Such assessments ask students to explain, interpret, apply, analyze, synthesize, solve problems, and communicate information.

ASSESSMENT BY EXHIBITION:
AN APPROACH TO ASSESSMENT

We believe that schools should define competencies all students need to fulfill in order to graduate from school, and then plan graduation exit exhibitions and portfolios that allow students to demonstrate that they've attained those competencies. One of the key components of this approach to curriculum design and implementation is the student exhibition or portfolio review as a means to assess student progress and achievement. Exhibitions are the projects or performances students present at culminating moments throughout their education. These exhibitions might occur at the end of a six-week unit, at midyear, or as a requirement for high school graduation. Exhibitions tie together all the work and competencies each student has mastered during a course of study and thus represent the complex process of curriculum development, instructional practice, and assessment in small schools.

Assessment asks students to demonstrate what they know and can do. Teachers gather this evidence throughout a unit of study or period of time and also in a final exhibition, culminating project, or performance. Very early in the curriculum development process, teachers think about ongoing and final assessments and how students might demonstrate their achievement of learning competencies. All assessments are challenging and are based on high expectations of both teachers and students.

A basic outline of the process leading to an exhibition is as follows:

1. Students are introduced to the exhibition assignment and are shown models or exemplars of what a successful exhibition looks like.

2. Using the models as a springboard, teacher and students develop criteria for the exhibition. These criteria may be extended into a rubric.

3. The teacher guides the students through the sequence of learning activities and product development that will lead to the exhibition. Students are given ample opportunity to receive feedback on their progress and at regular intervals are asked to reflect on their thinking and learning.

4. Drafts of work are critiqued by peers and teacher.

5. A final exhibition performance takes place with an audience of peers, teachers, and/or families.

From the beginning, students should have a clear understanding of what is expected of them in terms of the quality of their work and how their work will be evaluated. For example, teachers can use rubrics, develop assessment criteria with students, and display models of exemplary work to help students understand what is expected of them. Rather than just giving students a grade that tells them how they did in relation to each other or to an unidentified standard, teachers use assessments that give students feedback, and this feedback helps them improve. Assessment tasks that are based on clearly communicated learning competencies help students know what is important to learn and assist teachers in understanding the effectiveness of their teaching.

Characteristics of Effective Assessment

Effective assessment . . .

- Is transparent. Students know the criteria, learning goals, and timing of assessment.
- Drives curriculum planning and teaching. What students are asked to do depends on how they will be asked to demonstrate their learning.
- Takes many forms. There are a variety of assessments conducted in numerous ways.
- Includes reflection. Students are regularly asked to reflect on their learning, both in writing and in discussion with peers, teachers, and family members. They are taught to use metacognition—reflection on their own thinking and learning—to recognize when they are confused and to learn how to become "unstuck."
- Shows what students know and can do. Assessments help students, teachers, parents, and others understand what a student knows and can do, allow adults to understand what a student needs to improve.
- Is ongoing. Assessment is ongoing, tied to the learning goals, and used to inform curriculum planning, teaching, and professional development.

Sample Culminating Assessments from the Boston Pilot Schools

- In front of their peers, a teacher, and three outside evaluators from industry and the community, students present their solutions to math research questions. One student discusses the mathematical formula behind a card trick, another outlines the geometric progression of the rat population as it breeds, and a third student talks about the Cartesian coordinate system and its impact on the world. The reviewers ask questions and complete the rubric, which will ultimately affect the quarterly grade of all who present. (Fenway High School math exhibitions)

(Continued)

(Continued)

> - A student stands before an audience of teachers, family members, fellow students, and administrators to explain a topic she chose to research: How do blind people cope with living in a seeing world? She queries the audience, challenging their assumptions about the blind, and offers alternative ways of serving the disabled from around the world. Her presentation encompasses an investigation of literature and science related to blindness. After fifty minutes, the audience fills out feedback forms that will help guide the student's future work. (New Mission High School independent learning project presentation)

CREATING CURRICULUM THROUGH BACKWARDS DESIGN

Curricula should be designed with the end goal for learning in mind. This focus on "backwards design" often means creating the final assessment as an early step in curriculum unit planning. For example, a teacher or team of teachers may plan a mock election and a political speech as the final assessments of a six-week study of government. Initial planning questions should include, *What will an excellent mock election and an excellent written speech look like?* and, *What understandings, skills, and habits of mind will students demonstrate by successfully completing these assessments?* Given these assessments, and planning backwards, what is the appropriate sequence for the whole unit? Every step of the unit—every lesson, reading, mini-lecture, and activity—should prepare students for success in the final assessments. Much of the work of the unit will provide building blocks for the final assessments—research, drafts of writing, and practice performances. Learning competencies, an organizing theme, essential questions, and assessments are the four anchor points of a curriculum unit.

Learning competencies of a unit or course of study are a synthesis of the specific habits of mind, understandings, and skills that serve as the learning goals for that study.

- *Habits of mind*—the ways of thinking and being and acting that all students develop during the course of study.
- *Understandings*—a body of knowledge that is essential for all students to learn, understand, and apply. While it may be important at certain times for students to memorize and recall facts and information, it is critical that goals in this area include deeper understanding and application of knowledge. For example, knowledge of the events leading up to the American Revolution would be applied in an analysis of why the war began; an understanding of

the concept of fractions would involve an understanding of why it is important to know how to solve equations using fractions.

- *Skills*—What all students will be able to do by the end of a unit or course of study. Writing narratives, conducting research, using a keyboard, speaking a foreign language, and solving a complex problem are all examples of important skills. An important area of skill is product development—the ability to create products (different genres of writing, artwork, science fair models, etc.) that meet standards of quality and show evidence of learning.

Theme is the concept or "big idea" around which the study is centered. It should clearly reflect the learning competencies. It should also be a concept that is important to humanity and can be explored across disciplines, eras, and cultures. Power, balance, force, relationships, patterns, and freedom are all appropriate themes. Themes should engage students by being tied to their interests and concerns.

Essential questions help focus students on the most important aspects of the theme. Teachers and students consider two or three substantive questions throughout the unit and look at them from multiple perspectives. These questions lead to other questions that will engage students and deepen their inquiry.

Example of Theme and Essential Questions

Culture: Values and Beliefs

- What factors shape our values and beliefs?
- What happens when the belief systems of societies and individuals come into conflict?
- Are there universal characteristics of belief systems that are common across peoples and times?

CREATING A COHERENT SCHOOLWIDE CURRICULUM

The curriculum in a school should be coherent and develop from grade to grade in a progression that builds on the knowledge and skills learned in each grade. In order to build a coherent curriculum across their schools, teachers and administrators should create a curriculum map for the entire school. This process includes asking the following questions:

- What do we want our students to know and be able to do?
- What are the district and state standards?

- What are we currently teaching?
- Where are the redundancies and the gaps between what we should be teaching and what we are teaching?
- What will we do about the redundancies and gaps?

THE CENTRALITY OF LITERACY

What Is Literacy?

All too often literacy is viewed as the domain of the English/Language Arts teachers and is defined as a set of testable skills that is acquired in a linear fashion. We view literacy more broadly and emphasize engaging the student, connecting with families and the community, and building a collaborative culture for learning. Literacy is a social act. It is also a process of thinking, questioning, problem posing, and problem solving that is critical in every subject area. Literacy helps people take control of their lives. It is about respecting the knowledge already acquired by students. Literacy is a conversation: student to student, teacher to student, and student to teacher. It is about listening to students as they articulate what is meaningful to them and work to negotiate their relationship to their world.

To teach literacy, schools must recognize that all students have the capacity to make meaning and must ensure that they are held to high expectations and given equal opportunities to develop their literacy capacity. Schools must also recognize that teaching literacy is the responsibility of every teacher and must be embedded in the curriculum and structures of the school.

Schools can create a literate culture that will draw a student into another world of language, one formed by writing: books, short texts, student-created texts, and teacher writings. To engage students in becoming literate requires school and classroom structures and instructional strategies that actively engage students in things they care about, explicitly teach skills, and take into account the different backgrounds and experiences students bring with them.

Literacy and Democracy

There is a clear link between literacy and democracy. A strong civil society depends on the fair exchange of ideas among members of the democracy. Preparing students as readers and writers is preparing them to be participants in public discourse, negotiations, debate, consensus building, coalition formation, and other forms of public talk. As students learn to be active readers, writers, listeners, and speakers, we prepare them to be entrepreneurial in the broadest sense of the word—creative, independent thinkers—a quality that is much desired in this new century.

If schools are to be places where students prepare to be highly literate individuals, they must also be places where students are encouraged to be strong citizens, and that means participating in healthy debate. This view of literacy is closely related to habits of mind, as students practice the habits of being literate thinkers. Schools should be laboratories for democracy, where issues important to students' lives are actively debated, different viewpoints are articulated and considered, and every voice is encouraged. Through structures such as town meetings, student government, student publications, and community service projects, a culture of democracy can be created within a classroom or a school. It is within this culture of democracy that literacy flourishes, as students work to hone their skills and become better readers, writers, speakers, listeners, and thinkers.

Literacy and Thinking Across the Content Areas

A critical dimension of literacy in every subject area is developing the capacity to recognize when you are confused and what to do about it. Monitoring one's learning in any forum—reading history or science texts, solving algebraic equations, writing a persuasive essay, conducting a successful experiment—requires specific thinking strategies.

A student who uses such thinking strategies is engaged in a process of thinking and monitoring understanding that should go on throughout any challenging learning process. If an activity or assignment is so straightforward that it does not require a student to use any of these strategies, one could reasonably wonder whether it is worth doing.

Consider the following example from *Strategies That Work* (Harvey and Goudvis, 2000):

> Seventh-grade science teacher Margaret Bobb has developed an interesting form that supports synthesizing in the content areas. She uses a three-column Compare and Contrast note form. The first and third columns are headed with the content to be compared, in this case Kelp in the first column and Coral in the third column as Margaret explores marine biology with her students. The middle column is headed Alike. As Margaret and her students read, they record the properties of kelp in the first column and the properties of coral in the third. When they encounter similarities between the two, they record that information in the middle column. The middle column is a synthesis of the similarities between coral and kelp. (p. 149)

Now imagine that instead of teaching this strategy to her students, Margaret simply assigned the chapter on kelp and coral as homework reading and gave a quiz the next day. Many, if not most, students would let the information wash over them without comprehending or synthesizing it.

In a comparable math classroom, students of mixed levels of preparation are taught a repertoire of strategies to approach difficult problems: estimation, trial and error, cross-checking by using more than one way to do a problem, and smart use of tools (manipulatives, graphs, calculators, etc.). When a new concept is introduced, the class is noisy, as small groups of students help each other through an initial set of problems.

What does it look like when students use these strategies as an ongoing part of their learning and self-assessment? In the science class, students can use their journals or reading logs to engage in "quick writes," recording the central idea of a text and/or the strategies they use. In the math class, they can engage in similar problem analysis. What strategies did they use to solve the problems? When errors were made, what type of errors were they (e.g., "solving the wrong problem" or "careless mistake")? Sticky notes for responses and questions, copies of texts that can be marked up, and highlighting markers are all useful tools for this kind of reflection.

Tool 5.1: Guidelines for Developing Inquiry-Based Curriculum Units

Purpose: To assist teachers and others in developing inquiry-based curriculum.

Directions: Use these questions to guide curriculum design.

1. Theme

   What themes will students investigate?

2. Essential Question

   What essential question will guide student inquiry?

3. Learning Competencies

   Habits of mind: What ways of thinking and acting will students develop?

   Essential skills: What will all students be able to do as a result of this course of study?

   Content knowledge: What knowledge will all students possess by the end of this course of study?

4. Tools and Resources

   What materials and resources will be needed to create this course of study?

5. Culminating Project/Performance and Outcomes

   This process is also one students can use to create their own culminating project(s).

   - Brainstorm how people outside of the school use the habits of mind, skills, and content that all students will be learning.
   - Select one or more of these ideas and shape them into a culminating project or performance that students can do.
   - How will this project ask students to apply the habits of mind and the essential skills of the unit?
   - How will this project ask all students to demonstrate the new understanding of content they have developed through the unit?
   - What opportunities will there be for all students to do original work and/or develop new knowledge?
   - What public audience will all students have for demonstrating their learning from this unit?
   - What value does the project have beyond the assignment?

6. Sequence of Learning Experience

These guidelines map the sequence of learning experiences for the unit. Order the learning experiences you have selected to show the progression of the unit towards its culminating project. Map out a rough sequence, including major deadlines and important checkpoints of student understanding and skill development.

- The start of the unit should engage all students and spark their interest in the theme and essential questions.
- The expected learning competencies should be clear to all students from the beginning of the unit (this might be accomplished through discussion of competencies, students rewriting competencies in their own language, developing the competencies with students, and/or students deciding what evidence should show attainment of these learning competencies).
- Spend time determining what all students already know and are able to do in relation to the learning competencies.
- Determine what students should do for each activity. Standards of work should reflect higher-order thinking and be clear to all students (including the use of models, rubrics, assessment criteria, project timelines, and assignment requirements).
- Experiences that teach skills, habits of mind, and essential understandings should be organized so they build on one another and lead to the culminating performance or project.
- Instructional and learning methods should be varied. Students should have significant opportunities to make decisions and choices about their paths to mastery of the learning competencies addressed in the unit.
- Include both formal and informal checkpoints during the study to gauge student progress toward learning goals.

Student needs and interests checklist

Use these key questions to ensure that your unit will be clear to students.

- How will the work be organized and structured so students know what they have to do?
- What opportunities will students have for making decisions and choices about their learning?
- How will students know the standards for the work they do?

7. Ongoing Assessments

Formal: What formal work and assignments will show how students are doing as the unit progresses?

Informal: What informal observations and responses will demonstrate how students are doing as the course of study progresses?

8. Final Reflections and Self-Assessment

For students: Use these questions to create a reflection tool to guide students on their experience with this unit.

- What have you learned in this unit that has real meaning for you?
- Which assignment helped you learn the most?
- How will what you learned in this unit help you in other areas of life?
- What recommendations do you have to make this unit stronger?
- What advice do you have for future students who may study this unit?

For teachers: Use these questions to help teachers reflect on their experience teaching the unit.

- What worked well in planning this unit?
- What seemed to best engage all learners?
- What would I do differently if I were to teach this unit again?
- What did I learn from creating and teaching this unit that can be applied to the next unit?
- How will all students receive support needed for achieving the determined learning competencies?

DEVELOPING CURRICULUM, INSTRUCTION, AND
ASSESSMENT UNIT/COURSE OF STUDY

PLANNING GUIDE TEMPLATE

1. Theme	2. Essential Questions
What concept or big idea, tied to students' own interests and concerns, will this course of study be centered around?	What essential questions will drive student focus on key aspects of the theme and engage and guide student inquiry?

3. Learning Competencies

Habits of Mind	Content Knowledge	Skills
What ways of thinking, being, and acting will all students develop during this course of study?	What essential body of knowledge will all students have mastered at the end of this course of study?	What specific, essential skills will all students have mastered at the end of this course of study?

4. Tools and Resources

What materials and resources will be needed to create this course of study?

5. Culminating Project/Performance and Outcomes

What project or performance will ask all students to apply the knowledge, skills, and habits of mind developed through this course of study? How will each student demonstrate mastery of the unit's work and learning goals? What value will this course of study's learning have beyond the culminating project?

6. Sequence of Learning Experiences

How will the activities engage all students with the relevant content, skills, and habits of mind? How will these activities build toward the culminating assessment?

7. Ongoing Assessments

Formal:
What formal work and assignments will show how students are doing as the unit progresses?

Informal:
What informal observations and responses will demonstrate how students are doing as the course of study progresses?

8. Reflections and Self-Assessment

How will all students and teachers reflect on what worked well and what needs improvement?

SOURCES: Cushman, K. (1996). Developing curriculum in essential schools, *Horace, 12*(4), 1–12; Center for Collaborative Education. (2001). *Turning Points guide to curriculum development.* Boston: Author; Wiggins, G., & McTighe, J. (2001). *Understanding by design.* Alexandria, VA: Association for Supervision and Curriculum Development.

Restructuring the School for Personalization

The 1,600-student North High School was in the early planning stages for restructuring their large high school into small schools. The Planning Team—with representative membership from the faculty, administration, student body, and community—was meeting regularly. This team had already led and facilitated the process for creating a new vision for North High School, and the well-crafted statement was displayed throughout the school. Now it was time to get down to the nuts and bolts of school organization. Making the school smaller was a great idea, but how, exactly, would they divide up the students and teachers to make small schools? Who would be in charge of each small school? What schedule should they use? What would the new school budget look like?

The structures that guide a school community through its day-to-day operations—its master schedules, the length and frequency of class periods, how students and teachers are grouped, and how financial resources are allocated—reflect the beliefs and values of the school. If a school believes that all students learn in the same way and at the same pace, then traditional structures, in which all students attend classes for 42-minute periods and sit in rows to listen to teacher lectures, might make sense. However, when a school recognizes that students learn in different ways, and the school wants to provide learning opportunities to help all students succeed, traditional school structures need to be reexamined.

AUTHORS' NOTE: Portions of this chapter were previously published in CCE's Turning Points guides, *School Structures That Support Learning and Collaboration* (2001) and *At the Turning Point: The Young Adolescent Learner* (2003).

Small schools evaluate existing school structures to make sure they support the school community's vision about what it wants for its students by asking and answering questions such as the following:

- Does the way students are grouped allow all students access to rigorous learning opportunities?
- Do teachers have enough common planning time and other resources to create a curriculum that helps students develop habits of mind and the skills of intellectual inquiry?
- Do students and teachers have long enough blocks of time to engage in authentic intellectual work?
- Are budget decisions based upon a school's learning goals?

By consciously aligning organizational structures with underlying beliefs about students and schools, small schools foster higher student achievement and a positive collaborative culture among students and teachers alike.

Creating a culture of authentic learning in small, democratic communities is essential to improved student performance and achievement. Students need caring communities that both support and challenge them academically. Small schools create organizational structures to guide them on their journey to improved student learning and achievement. Guided by the principles of effective small schools and their own vision statements, the schools figure out which structures would best meet their own needs.

THE INTERCONNECTEDNESS OF SCHOOL STRUCTURES

Schedules, student groupings, and allocation of resources are often the most entrenched aspects of a learning community, creating a complex weave of interdependent elements. Making one change in a school can quickly affect the entire foundation. For example, when a school decides to have its ninth-grade students present cumulative portfolios as part of an end-of-year requirement, it may find itself redesigning the master schedule so that teachers have more advisory time with their students to help them develop their portfolios. For structural change to be effective, schools need to take into account all the interrelated factors involved in making the change, rather than proceeding in a piecemeal fashion.

This interconnectedness can be viewed as a strength because it allows schools to function as one unified system. A unified system enables educators to recognize patterns and relationships, to develop continuity among a myriad of projects and initiatives, and thus to learn more effective ways of structuring itself. However, for some this complexity can be overwhelming, causing a reluctance to change anything for fear of disrupting the whole system. Careful planning and ensuring that the whole school community is informed and involved are critical to successful structural change.

When seeking to make change within a school, such as improving student achievement or developing a collaborative culture among colleagues, educators often look first at the school's structures. Structures alone, however, do not improve a school or student achievement. Rather, they create the conditions for more effective teaching and learning. While some may think that changing the schedule is easier than changing the underlying beliefs or norms that cause the school to function as it does, a combination of factors is usually at work when a school shows real and lasting improvement. Real improvements can be seen only when a structural change is accompanied by a clearly defined vision to improve student learning, faculty ownership of the process and commitment to developing a deeper understanding of teaching and learning, and ample resources allocated to support change.

Before Cynthia Ortiz became the director of a small school, one of the major dilemmas she faced as a school principal was that, while she could identify what her students and their families needed, she was not able to access the necessary resources through the centralized bureaucracy of her large urban school system. She understood district resources were limited, but she also knew there were better ways to allocate them to match the particular needs of her school. Converting to a small school was a move in the right direction: it allowed her and her staff to have increased autonomy over their resources—budget, staffing, and scheduling. Being able to make decisions about resources in order to make a difference for students and families and to improve the working conditions for teachers was empowering for everyone.

PERSONALIZATION THROUGH AUTONOMIES OF BUDGET, STAFFING, AND CALENDAR

Research suggests that when schools are able to meet two conditions—creating environments where students are well known to their teachers and providing teachers with adequate time to collaborate—they are more successful in meeting the needs of their students (Miles-Hawley & Darling-Hammond, 1998). The challenge for schools in creating these conditions lies in using their limited resources of money, people, and time. Small schools should have the autonomies necessary to create unified learning communities and use their resources to provide personalized, high-quality teaching and learning for all students.

Using Budget and Staffing to Meet Student Needs

School reform to improve teaching and learning does not always require additional funding. While grants can provide new funding sources for coaching and professional development on a short-term basis, schools that are interested in long-term, sustainable reform need to rethink how they allocate the resources already available to them. These resources include money, staffing, and time.

Reallocating resources always requires trade-offs and can trigger difficult changes for schools. If a school decides that it wants to lower its student-teacher ratio by transitioning to an in-class model of special education academic support, or lower teachers' student loads by creating two-person teams, individuals will inevitably be affected. While these sorts of decisions should be consensual among the faculty, school leaders should be mindful that change is difficult, both logistically and personally. Giving individual teachers time to make decisions, to transition, and to develop new skills is essential to making effective changes (Miles-Hawley & Hornbeck, 2000).

Sample Ways to Use Budget and Staffing Resources

Reduce student-teacher loads: Adopt a longer block schedule in order to create more sustained learning time and to lower student-teacher loads. Alternately, designate humanities teachers instead of separate English and history teachers, thereby enabling the student-teacher load for humanities to be halved.

Decrease class size: Allocate as many positions as possible to the teachers in core academic programs, thereby decreasing class size in these courses.

Special education teachers: Use in-class consultation models for academic support by placing special education teachers in regular classrooms with their colleagues instead of in a resource room.

Title I teachers and funding: Staff Title I teachers as regular classroom teachers. Title I teachers can also serve as team-based or schoolwide instructional facilitators. Use Title I funds for school-based professional development.

Two-person academic teams: Reduce student-teacher ratios by organizing teachers into two-person teams.

Substitute teachers: Use substitute teachers to free up team teachers for common planning time to work on curriculum and develop coherence across grades.

Administrative staff: Streamline administrative staff, shifting roles to instructional facilitators and literacy and math specialists.

Professional development conferences: Approve teacher attendance at conferences only when the conference content supports the school's professional development goals.

School-based professional development: Use full-faculty meeting time to create two- to three-hour blocks for professional development and study groups. Use common planning time among team teachers for professional development. As much as possible, save business items for written communication.

Make teachers generalists: Have teachers also serve as advisors, thereby further personalizing learning for every student.

Organizing Time to Support Learning: Time as a Resource and Scheduling as a Tool

When the focus of a school is on improving student learning, problems begin to surface with a scheduling structure of seven or eight 42-minute classes a day. The 42-minute class period in separate subject areas provides limited opportunities to accommodate the diverse learning styles of students or to engage them in meaningful, authentic work. The amount of class time allotted is always the same, regardless of the complexity of the material, project, or subject area. Interdisciplinary connections among subject areas are superficial at best. Time spent passing between and settling into classes is lost potential learning time.

When the focus of a school's change effort is on improving student learning, time becomes a resource, and scheduling becomes a tool by which to more effectively serve students. However, lengthening class periods or making other changes in the school schedule alone will not improve student learning (Canady & Rettig, 1995). Teachers need to develop a curriculum and adopt teaching practices that provide students with meaningful and authentic learning experiences.

Guidelines for Using Time to Support Learning

- *Student learning time.* Longer blocks of instructional time allow students and teachers to delve more deeply into learning experiences than the traditional 42-minute period allows. Instead of the class period coming abruptly to an end, students and teachers can let lively discussions about a book they're reading or a social issue they're examining come to a natural end. Students can make real progress on group projects or labs. When students have the time to understand new concepts and apply what they've learned, they are more apt to retain information. Teachers can change student groupings multiple times in one learning block according to students' interests and diverse learning needs. In longer learning blocks, teachers can use time creatively to increase student learning.

- ***Flexibility in scheduling.*** Flexibility in scheduling allows academic teams to use the blocks of time to best serve their learning purposes. For example, a science/math teacher in a two-person team may want to use the time to work with students on a project for a whole week. Or a team might want to create a United Nations conference for an entire day. Teacher teams should be in charge of dividing their own blocks of time to best suit instructional purposes.

- ***Common planning time for academic teams.*** There should be ample common planning time for the members of academic teams to develop an interdisciplinary curriculum that focuses on essential questions, to use protocols for looking at student and teacher work, and to meet with parents. Lack of common planning time for teachers has emerged as one of the key deterrents to achieving effective school change. Schools must find ways to provide enough time for teachers to work together to improve their practice.

- ***Include specialty-subject teachers.*** Finding ways for teachers of specialty subjects such as art and physical education to participate as team teachers is challenging. Often these teachers meet with many more students than team teachers and need to teach while team teachers have common planning time. Rotate specialty-subject teachers' schedules each term so that they can join at least one team per term. In this way, specialty-subject teachers share common planning time with team teachers and meet to discuss students, look at student work, and plan an interdisciplinary curriculum.

- ***Interface with support and non-teaching staff.*** Because there is usually a network of adults supporting students, it is important to include these staff members in team meetings. One possibility is to rotate the weekly agenda of team meetings so that each day's meeting includes the appropriate staff. For example, one day might focus on special education or differentiated instruction in the classroom, in which case the special education teacher should be present, if he or she is not already a core team teacher. Another meeting day might be dedicated to teamwide curriculum planning, in which case the director of instruction or the community service coordinator might participate.

Sample Ways Schools Find Time for Faculty to Work Together

Here are some ways schools have found time for collaborative work (Murphy, 1997):

- Negotiate with the district to claim all district early-release time for school-based professional development.
- Shift to longer blocks of learning time to increase instructional time and reduce time spent in the hallways between classes.
- Release students early one day a week.
- Use teacher assistants to release teachers for one-hour study group meetings.
- Use teams of parents and/or business partners to release teachers for meetings.
- One day a week, begin school thirty minutes later and ask teachers to come in thirty minutes earlier to create a one-hour block of meeting time.
- Hire a team of substitute teachers to spend a day every other week at the school in order to release groups of teachers for collaborative work.
- Schedule "special enrichment assemblies" for students to provide time for teachers to meet.
- Limit meetings of the full faculty to one day a month.
- Compensate teachers for collaborative work done after school.
- Start school five minutes early and end five minutes later Tuesdays through Fridays. This creates forty minutes of faculty meeting time that can be added to each Monday.
- Shorten required afterschool time for teachers four days a week to create a longer block of meeting time after school one day a week.
- Use a team of college or university students to free teachers for collaborative work.
- Create regular common planning time for academic teams or study groups by sending all students in a cluster or grade level to specialists during a designated period.

Sample Schedules

Flexible Block Schedule. This model works for either a four-person or a two-person team. The chart below shows the schedule that one group of students would follow. Sample A requires the team teachers to divide the morning block of time as they see fit. This ensures maximum ownership and flexibility. While students are taking specialty subjects, the core teachers have common planning time. In this scenario, specialty subject teachers are available to participate in common planning time two or three days per week. The academic team teachers can meet from 12:45 PM to 2:30 PM on Tuesdays, Wednesdays, and Thursdays, and from 1:40 PM to 2:30 PM on Mondays and Fridays. Fifteen extra minutes are built into the morning block to allow for settling in, daily attendance, announcements, a mid-morning break, and/or passing time.

Sample A: Flexible Block Schedule

	Monday	*Tuesday*	*Wednesday*	*Thursday*	*Friday*
8:25–12:00 (215 min.)	Core Block	Core Block	Core Block	Core Block	Core Block
12:05–12:40 (35 min.)	Lunch	Lunch	Lunch	Lunch	Lunch
12:45–1:35 (50 min.)	Advisory	Gym	Music	Gym	Advisory
1:40–2:30 (50 min.)	Spanish	Spanish	Spanish	Spanish	Spanish

A/B Schedule. This model works for either several small schools within a larger school building or a single school (either stand-alone or part of a larger school building). The premise of this schedule is to allow for longer blocks of time (in this case 90 minutes) for students and teachers to engage in substantive learning experiences. Classes meet every other day. Teachers see a smaller number of students each day, and students take a smaller course load on the "A" and "B" days. Additionally, teachers within the small school could schedule common planning times during their open blocks; each teacher in the small school would teach or team-teach during two or three of each day's blocks. Days of the week are not assigned; rather, "B" always follows "A," taking into account holidays and inservice days.

Sample B: A/B Schedule

Time	*"A" Days*	*"B" Days*
8:00–9:30	Period 1	Period 2
9:35–11:05	Period 3	Period 4
11:10–1:15	Period 5 and lunch: one half of the students have lunch for 35 minutes at the beginning of the period; the other half have lunch for 35 minutes at the end.	Period 6 and lunch: one half of the students have lunch for 35 minutes at the beginning of the period; the other half have lunch for 35 minutes at the end.
1:20–2:50	Period 7	Period 8

GROUPING STUDENTS FOR LEARNING

A small school has a defined physical area with a dedicated administration, a faculty small enough to work together collaboratively, a student body numbering anywhere between 50 and 400 students, and student-teacher ratios of not more than 80:1 at the secondary level and 20:1 at the elementary level. Schools make different decisions about how to configure their student populations, depending on the existing size and location of the school and its student body. They need to develop policies for student enrollment and figure out how to group the students within the building and within classrooms so that all students receive the benefits of personalization and low student-teacher ratios that small schools can provide.

Developing Policies for Student Enrollment

Developing policies for student enrollment in small schools can create dilemmas for the governing bodies of small schools. Small schools are shown to be more successful when staff is self-selected and students volunteer to enroll. And because students choose to enroll in a particular small school, usually due to the focus of the school program, their parents tend to be more involved, thus boosting the academic achievement of their sons and daughters.

However, school governing bodies must take great care to avoid creating a system of "haves and have-nots" within a school district by attracting only the most motivated students and cooperative families, or a disproportionately higher percentage of affluent or White students, to the small school environment. Enrollment policies should show the school's intention to benefit all students in a community by requiring a balanced representation of all students in the district. The student enrollment of a small school must be both a result of student and parent choice and a reflection of equitable representation across the entire school district by race, ethnicity, income status, gender, language, and special education status.

Looping and Multiage Grouping

Within small schools, students and teachers can be grouped to promote longer and more meaningful student-teacher relationships. Alternatives to grouping by grade level include looping and multiage grouping. Looping means keeping the same students and teachers together for more than one year. With multiage grouping, students at more than one grade level are together in a class. Most multiage classes are looped. The practices of looping and multiage grouping can greatly increase opportunities for building relationships and addressing the learning needs of all students.

Looping is the practice of having the same students and teachers work together over multiple years. Some schools group students and teachers for two years (e.g., ninth and tenth grades only), while in other schools students and teachers work together for their entire tenure.

The Benefits of Looping

- *Positive Relationship*. Students have the opportunity to develop relationships over a longer period of time. Similarly, parents and teachers get to know each other over the course of more than one year and are able to build richer and more fruitful relationships.
- *More time for teaching and learning.* The pacing in the second year tends to be faster because teachers build on previous skills and knowledge, going deeper into topics and moving more quickly. Because teachers know their students well, less time is spent on review and preassessment of students' skills and knowledge, and more time is spent on in-depth learning experiences.
- *Fewer behavior problems.* Teachers find they have more positive interactions with students, while discipline and behavior management requirements decrease. This climate encourages intellectual risk taking and greater involvement of students. Students benefit from time spent developing social skills and cooperative group strategies.
- *Interpersonal conflict resolution*. When a teacher and a student clash in single-year groupings, there is less incentive to work through the problem. Looping gives teachers the incentive to work harder to reach students; likewise, it gives students the incentive to work through problems and conflicts.
- *Reduction in grade retention*. Looping can reduce grade retention because it provides students with the chance to raise achievement over the course of two years rather than just one.
- *Student confidence.* Individual students respond to the increased intimacy by participating more actively and feeling greater confidence and pride in being part of a group. Students tend to feel less nervous and apprehensive beginning the school year, particularly their second or subsequent years with a group.

The Challenges to Looping

- *Unsuccessful groups.* While looping does afford a group the opportunity to grow and develop together, if the chemistry of the group is not working or if the group development process is not effective, students as well as teachers can feel "stuck with each other"—not for one year, but for two or more years. Clear guidelines for moving students and reforming groups at the end of the year can solve this challenge.

- *Professional development.* Teachers new to this method need support, reinforcement of content knowledge, planning time, and mentorship to set goals for individual students and develop an effective curriculum over two years or more.

Multiage Grouping

In a multiage group, students of two (or more) grade levels are together in each class. At the end of each year, older students move on and a new class of younger students moves up a grade to join the group. Multiage groups are typically looped, meaning that students stay with the same teachers for more than one year.

Benefits of Multiage Grouping

- *Social and academic flexibility.* More social and academic flexibility is possible for students who are more advanced in some areas than in others. For example, a student may be socially mature but weak in a particular academic area.
- *Heterogeneous grouping.* Multiage grouping supports heterogeneity and encourages leadership and confidence building among all students. There are opportunities for students to take on leadership roles beyond academics. Students can model effective behaviors in groups and in other ways important to learning.
- *Student responsibility for learning.* Multiage grouping increases students' responsibility for their learning, since students are encouraged to learn at their own level and pace.
- *Students as mentors.* Multiage grouping provides opportunities for older students to mentor younger students. There is always a group of students who are familiar with the class routines and who can act as role models for the new and younger students. In this regard, learning is reinforced through students teaching students, rather than just the teachers teaching.
- *Less competition.* Multiage grouping diminishes competition among students because it breaks down "class" structures between older and younger students and limits the arbitrary privileging of older students.

Challenges to Multiage Grouping

- *Professional development.* Professional development is needed for teachers in the areas of building content knowledge and developing varied instructional approaches. Because many teachers are unfamiliar with multiage grouping, a school may benefit from providing mentorships and other forms of support for teachers.

- *Allocating and providing resources.* The wide developmental range of students in a multiage class requires schools to rethink how they assign existing staff such as aides, specialists, reading tutors, or student teachers.

- *Family support and buy-in.* Many families are unfamiliar with the benefits of multiage groups, and they may be uncomfortable with this structure. It is important for schools to provide adequate information to parents about multiage groupings, as well as to plan a transition period during which concerned students and their families can adapt to the new structure.

Heterogeneous Learning Groups

As small schools seek to create school cultures that encourage and support high achievement for all students, they abandon traditional "tracking" systems that place students in learning groups according to academic achievement as measured by standardized tests, teacher recommendation, or other predetermined criteria. Tracking is the practice of grouping students for long periods of time according to perceived ability, with little or no flexibility for changing student needs and performance.

Separating students into groups according to their perceived academic abilities and achievement (homogeneous grouping) weakens the learning experience for everyone. Often, such student groupings are informed by a hierarchy that suggests students must master a certain set of skills and content before moving on to another level. Students placed in lower tracks seldom find the opportunities to move on to classes in which they are appropriately challenged to use advanced skills and content (Wheelock, 1992).

With students of color and economically disadvantaged youth often placed disproportionately in the lower tracks, the achievement gap widens (Oakes, 1985). Tracking reinforces racial and social isolation—a damaging proposition at any age, but especially as adolescents are developing (and making lasting decisions about) their sense of identity and place in the world. Students placed in low and advanced tracks often spend their school years with the same group of students, losing out on opportunities to know and learn from other students.

Instead, small schools place students in heterogeneous learning groups that reflect the learning characteristics of all students, including learning style, academic achievement, personal interests, and prior knowledge.

Benefits to Heterogeneous Grouping

- *High expectations for all students.* Small schools, with their commitment to equity and excellence, group their students heterogeneously so that everyone benefits. Students traditionally labeled as "low achievers" are held to the same high expectations as the "advanced" students. As expectations for their work moves beyond fill-in-the-blank exercises to authentic learning experiences that require critical thinking, low achievers are challenged and motivated to achieve at higher levels.

- *Access to challenging curriculum and instruction for all students.* All students have greater opportunities to learn. Students who have traditionally held places in higher tracks are expected to perform to high standards in heterogeneously grouped classes. They are assessed on their demonstrated skill level and knowledge rather than on the perceived level of their ability, which was often determined years earlier.

- *Varied and individualized instruction.* Higher-track students in homogeneous settings are often underchallenged because instruction is not individualized and does not offer varied approaches that push students to learn in new ways and develop critical thinking skills. Similarly, lower-track students often do not perform at higher levels because they are given assignments that are not challenging. A heterogeneous class allows teachers to draw upon all students' particular strengths and "intelligences" to create a rich learning environment.

- *Students learning from each other.* Students with all learning styles and levels of achievement have much to learn from the insights and experiences of their classmates as they engage in collaborative discourse and intellectual inquiry on topics of interest to them. In heterogeneously grouped classrooms, instruction is differentiated to reflect the varied learning needs of each student.

Differentiated Instruction in the Heterogeneously Grouped Classes

Simply putting a diverse group of students in a classroom does not ensure that significant learning will take place. Providing challenging content and a variety of learning strategies so that all students are able to understand and make connections with the content is essential. Using a differentiated instructional approach is an effective means for addressing the needs of each learner. In a school where teachers have small class sizes and no more than eighty students total, teachers can develop a range of instructional practices that allows for differentiation and modification based on students' needs.

Teachers usually differentiate their instruction in one of three ways: by task, by activity, or by assessment. When differentiating by activity, the task and means for assessment remain consistent for all students, but the activities that lead to completion of the task vary depending on the learner. A teacher may assign all students the same task—for example, writing a children's story. However, she may differentiate the activities so that all students are successful at completing the task. Some students may have an individual conference, some may meet to peer critique each others' drafts, and others may work in a small group with the special education teacher on a storyboard template that helps them develop their plot ideas. In this example, when the teacher assesses these students' stories, she uses the same rubric for all students. Knowing students well allows teachers to create the varied and differentiated instruction that helps all students achieve at high levels.

In differentiating instruction by task or assessment, a teacher might, for example, ask students to respond in different ways to a piece of literature they all have read. They might demonstrate their understanding of a character's motivations in a novel by acting out a scene from the story, writing an interpretive essay, or creating an outline for a sequel to the novel.

Practices such as project-based learning, reading and writing workshops, and well-structured and flexible cooperative learning groups can help motivate students to become active, responsible learners. Both teachers and students need training in how to utilize a variety of such learning strategies, and some students will still require additional support.

Guidelines for Teaching and Learning in a Heterogeneously Grouped Classroom

- ***Differentiated instruction:*** Vary instruction in ways that address individual learning needs. Differentiating instruction by task, activity, or assessment affords teachers the flexibility to meet the different learning needs of all students.

- ***Flexible groupings:*** Group students according to their learning needs and the requirements of the content or activity presented. At times it is appropriate to have short-term groupings of students for specific purposes, such as building basic numeracy and literacy skills.

- ***Collaborative work:*** Engage students in collaborative learning experiences. Encourage student input in making decisions about what and how to teach and learn. Use a variety of strategies for learning and teaching, including cooperative learning groups, project-based learning, peer tutoring, and process writing.

- ***Training in differentiated classroom practices:*** As schools move from homogeneous to heterogeneous groupings of students, both teachers and students need to be trained in new strategies for learning. For teachers, this requires an initial investment of time and effort through professional development opportunities inside and outside the classroom, along with a good dose of trial and error.

- ***Additional support and enrichment for students:*** When necessary, provide additional support and enrichment opportunities for students by using additional staff (instructional aides, special education staff, etc.) in the classroom. Students may also benefit from mentoring programs and cross-age tutoring, or from afterschool and Saturday homework centers.

ADVISORY AND STUDENT SUPPORT MODELS

Effective small schools need to create environments that promote personalized, caring relationships between adults and students and provide opportunities for these relationships to develop and flourish. Such relationships support and reinforce student learning and help students to grow into productive, responsible adults. A strong correlation exists between a student's academic success and having a close, personal relationship with at least one adult in the school. There are numerous ways that individual teachers create caring and personalized environments in their classrooms every day. Advisory programs provide a way for a school as a whole to support meaningful relationships between students and adults.

Advisory initiatives in small schools often take the form of structured programs that meet at specific times during the week. In advisory programs, groups of ten to fifteen students meet regularly with an adult, usually during the school day. Students stay with the same advisor at least two years and often throughout their tenure at the school.

Providing ample time for students and adults to interact informally and naturally around subjects of interest to them is essential. Student-adult relationships can grow when adults work with small groups of students during learning experiences in the classroom, on service projects within the community, or in special-interest clubs. In small schools, both structured programs and informal opportunities should exist for building relationships.

Examples of How Schools Use Advisory Time

- ***Working with students on academic issues.*** During a scheduled advisory period, students explore school-related issues such as developing study skills and individual learning plans, learning to use the library/resource center, planning for college, and learning peer mediation skills.

- ***Working to help the community.*** Groups of students and adults form service organizations to help the community by providing services to local senior centers, parks, libraries, etc.
- ***Working within the school community.*** Adult advisors help students gain workplace skills, such as planning and collaborating to provide a useful service to the school community. For example, one group of students experienced in technology may help their peers learn computer skills, while another takes part in a program to read to elementary students.
- ***Discussing social and developmental issues.*** Trained adults facilitate discussions with students about social and developmental issues and about concerns of adolescents such as peer and family relationships, health care, nutrition, and career planning.
- ***Sharing common interests.*** Students and teachers interact informally around a shared interest such as a craft, hobby, sport, or academic field.

TOOLS FOR RESTRUCTURING
THE SCHOOL FOR PERSONALIZATION

Tool 6.1: Guidelines for Differentiating Instruction

Purpose: To provide guidelines helpful in managing a differentiated classroom.

Guideline	Explanation
Have a strong rationale	Base your rationale for differentiating instruction on students' readiness and interest. Share that rationale with both students and parents so they can begin to understand the nature of a differentiated classroom and lose preconceived notions.
Begin differentiating at a comfortable pace	The teacher also has a level of readiness that needs to be considered. For example, teachers can try differentiated instruction in the class where they feel most at ease or with the subject they enjoy best. They can differentiate using multiple resources or have students work from a single text but at different paces.
Time activities for student success	Some students work better in groups, while others work better independently. All students should learn to increase their attention span for either group or independent work. For example, the teacher might first give the student just a little less time for an independent activity than her attention span typically allows. Starting with a shorter time frame allows the student's attention to outlast the task and gives her a sense of success. Then, gradually, the time allotted for similar tasks should increase.
Use "anchor" activities	Anchor activities free up time to work with students. Reading silently, writing in journals, and practicing skills allow students to work independently and quietly. These anchor tasks should be differentiated based on students' levels of readiness and interest. Gradually, teachers can move toward having part of the class involved in anchor activities, while others are involved in newer differentiated tasks that require more teacher attention.
Be strategic when delivering instructions	Since students will be engaged in different activities at the same time, avoid giving directions orally. Instead, prepare task cards or activity sheets, give instructions to group representatives, or set up learning stations with instructions readily available.

(Continued)

(Continued)

Guideline	Explanation
Have a "home base"	Basically, this is a seating chart students use at different times during the class to allow the teacher to organize lessons and materials more quickly.
Share responsibilities with students	Giving students as much responsibility for their learning as possible encourages them to become more independent and motivated learners. This includes distributing and collecting materials, organizing the classroom itself for various activities, reviewing peers' work, establishing goals for their own learning, and developing some of their own tasks.
Have a plan for students to get help	Students need to know how to get help when the teacher is busy with another student or group. Possibilities include asking for help from others in their group and putting their name on a list kept next to the teacher.
Set norms with students	Engage students in talking about classroom procedures that support learning.
Use flexible groupings	This means sometimes grouping students based on their level of readiness, interests, or learning profiles; sometimes having students work on a brief task with whoever is nearby; and sometimes allowing students to set up their own groups. These changes in grouping strategies prevent the implicit labeling of long-running groups.

SOURCE: Adapted from Jackson, A. W., & Davis, G. A. (2000). *Turning Points 2000* (New York: Teachers College Press), 80 [citing C. A. Tomlinson (1995), *The Differentiated Classroom* (Alexandria, VA: Association for Supervision and Curriculum Development), 29–33].

Tool 6.2: Advisory Design Checklist

Purpose: To provide areas for an Advisory Design Team to keep in mind when planning advisory programs.

FIRST STEPS

We have . . .

____ Formed a team of teachers, parents, community members, and administrators who will do the preliminary work on advisory

____ Allocated sufficient time for this team to do its work (6–12 months)

____ Created a realistic working timeline that recognizes the time needed for this team to
  • research
  • visit and talk to other schools that have or are creating advisories
  • meet regularly as a team
  • communicate with the rest of the school and community in ways designed to build support and interest in advisories

____ Allocated funding and time for professional development for advisors

____ Outlined how the advisory program will be phased in (whole school or pilot grades)

DESIGN

Our design has . . .

____ Clear goals and rationales as to why we are doing this work

____ Goals and rationales for specific grade levels

____ Expected outcomes for advisees, advisory groups, and school climate and culture

____ Point people with defined authority and responsibilities who will coordinate the advisory program and offer support and/or supervision to advisors as needed

____ A clear and workable schedule around length and frequency of sessions, allowing sufficient time to meet goals and outcomes

____ Grouping arrangements that allow for appropriate group size, student mix, and student-teacher continuity

___ Content and themes that support our goals

___ Routines, formats, and style of advisory groups

___ Clear advisor roles in terms of
- academic advising, report cards, and progress reports
- exhibitions and portfolios
- parent contact
- discipline
- career and college preparation
- school business and school involvement
- referrals for tutoring, counseling, health, and other needs

___ Professional development scheduled prior to launching advisories and ongoing for the first year

___ Materials and resources are available for advisors

___ Identified accountability processes that will
- influence students and advisors to take advisory seriously and participate effectively
- document outcomes
- allow for student, teacher, and parent reflection on advisory effectiveness
- assess the advisory program's impact on identified goals

___ Established advisory time as sacred time, free from fear of being "bumped"

SOURCE: Adapted from Poliner, R., & Lieber, C. M. (2004). *The Advisory Guide*. Cambridge, MA: Educators for Social Responsibility.

7

Building a Culture of Adult Learning and Collaboration

Jack Maloney, a teacher at a small school, was concerned about the uneven student attendance in his classes. He decided to bring up the issue at his monthly Critical Friends Group (CFG) meeting. To prepare for the meeting, Jack looked up student attendance in each of the classes for the members of this CFG. In doing this, the "problem" of school attendance became immediately personalized. His focusing questions were the following: Why do we have uneven attendance in many of our classes? Once we understand the reasons for uneven attendance, what can we do to improve it?

Teachers talked about existing school policies and interventions, but soon realized that there was no consistency in the message or approach. Each teacher handled the issue differently, and in fact, some teachers did not know whether there was a policy at all. Individual cases were discussed, and the notion of applying the same rule to everyone was also raised as a dilemma. For a school that works with older students, most of whom have adult responsibilities, such as children and work after school, "sticking to the guidelines" across the board presented difficulties in reaching consensus.

After several clarifying and probing questions, the members of the CFG then began to discuss possibilities. Some of the ideas that came out of the conversation were: entering into a contract with students with a high number of absences, creating a reward/award system for students with improved attendance, tying class credits to attendance, creating a "buddy" system, more actively involving students' families, inviting family members to meet at the school, maintaining logs of contact with the families, and addressing the issue with students during advisories.

AUTHOR'S NOTE: Portions of this chapter were previously published in CCE's Turning Points guide, *Guide to Collaborative Culture and Shared Leadership* (2001).

In debriefing the exercise, everyone agreed that approaching the problem with real data that each teacher could recognize as his/her own was a good starting point. The data immediately became personal, and the teacher could attach a person to the instances of tardiness or absences on the sheet. Beyond the numbers, the teacher could access personal stories and reasons for a particular student's absences and/or excellent participation and attendance. In looking at the data, which then became stories, the teachers were able to discuss ideas for a solution.

CREATING A PROFESSIONAL COLLABORATIVE CULTURE

Central to our philosophy is the idea that principals and teachers must have a commitment to the whole school in order to create and develop a tone of decency and trust. Reflective, collaborative work is key to the focus on teaching and learning in the school. Problems, such as the attendance issue above, must be discussed openly, with teachers and principals working together to solve them. Working together to improve student learning is the hallmark of the professional collaborative cultures in many small schools.

What Is School Culture?

Every school has its own culture. You can sense it as soon as you step inside the building, or sometimes even from the parking lot. Is the building well maintained? Are parents milling around and talking? Inside, is student work displayed on the walls? What about the tone of the school: is it cheerful, somber, chaotic? Do you feel welcomed as you enter? Are the doors to the administrative offices open? Are there parents in the building? How do students move through the hallways? How do they treat each other? What are they doing in the classrooms? What kinds of interactions take place between students and teachers? In the staff meeting rooms, what are the teachers working on and talking about?

Through these details, a school's culture is revealed. All these interwoven elements—how members of a school community teach and learn from each other, interact, communicate, express themselves, work together, reflect on their practice, and celebrate—form the rich fabric of school culture. There is much to learn from the daily life of a school. A community's core values and beliefs about the purpose of its school underlie and inform all that occurs there.

Where Does a School's Culture Come From?

Whether consciously built or not, a culture exists within every school. This culture comes from the attitudes and beliefs of the people who work and learn inside the school, the cultural norms that have always guided how the school operates, and the relationships among people there. But school culture is also the result of external influences. Outside factors from the local school district and community, and from society at large, have a significant impact on how the school works.

Often these cultural influences, both inside and outside the school, work against reform: an uninformed public questions the need for change; skeptics in the district offices and even within the school undermine the change effort; resentment surfaces among those who favor reform and those who do not. If the culture of the school is "don't fix what isn't broke" or "let's just jump on to the next bandwagon of reform in order to get more resources," the reform effort won't get the commitment necessary for success. Meaningful as opposed to superficial and episodic reform requires building a culture to sustain and embrace it, a culture that involves and engages teachers in decision making about key educational matters and new approaches to learning and teaching. In order to achieve lasting reform, teachers and others in the school community need to go beyond learning to work together in teams, create interdisciplinary curriculum units, or examine issues in study groups. They need time to understand and integrate the research-based principles of learning and teaching that underlie successful schools.

When schools seek to improve, a focus on the values, beliefs, and norms of both the school and the environment outside the school is necessary. School culture does not exist in a vacuum. It is created by internal and external forces and thus can be manipulated and changed to improve the school.

Different Types of School Cultures

School cultures vary widely from school to school: from the hierarchical and bureaucratic organizational structures that characterized most public school systems in the last century to the newly developing professional collaborative cultures of today. As schools move to build new cultures that are more effective in improving student learning, it is helpful to take a look at the chart below and assess where your school would be placed on this continuum.

Sample Continuum of School Cultures

The following chart provides a general overview of types of school governance and decision making, as well as of instruction, curriculum, and assessment. Schools may have components of several areas.

Table 7.1   Types of School Cultures

Type of Culture	School Governance	Instruction, Curriculum, Assessment, and Decision Making
Hierarchical and bureaucratic	Centralized decision making by a small group of administrators, with little or no teacher input. Teacher autonomy within the classroom, with restricted participation in schoolwide organizational and curricular decisions.	Defined by state and district specialists. Testing used to sort students homogeneously (by grade levels, for programs, in classroom groups). Teacher's job is to present a prescribed set of content and skills. Individual teachers are held accountable for student failure.
Noncollaborative: "Balkanization"	Separate and competing groups seek power for their own ends.	Poor integration of curriculum and instructional goals. Atmosphere of competition among teachers.
Noncollaborative: "Comfortable collaboration"	Comfortable, easygoing atmosphere is pleasant but does not solve troublesome issues facing the school community.	Teachers share some ideas, techniques, and materials to improve teaching and learning, but avoid deeper issues that impact curriculum and long-range planning.
Noncollaborative: "Contrived collegiality"	Formal, but not necessarily collaborative, structures (such as site-based management councils, school improvement teams, peer coaching) are in place and enable teachers to work together.	Work appears collaborative on the surface but doesn't translate into the deeper, more significant and productive practices found in collaborative settings.
Professional collaborative culture	Principal is a facilitative leader. Teachers have significant involvement in decision making. Teachers and students collaborate on issues that affect the whole school.	Significant teacher involvement in decision making about school goals, curriculum, and instructional practices. Collective responsibility for student achievement.

SOURCES: Fullan & Hargreaves (1991), Little (1990).

Successful Schools and School Culture

Research over the last three decades has identified several key characteristics of successful schools. These characteristics, also evident in schools with professional collaborative cultures, include

- A clear and focused vision
- High expectations for all students
- Purposeful and meaningful work
- Positive home-school connections
- A learning community small enough so that each student is known well by at least one adult

More recent and ongoing research into school culture adds collegiality and professional collaboration to the list (Levine & Lezotte, 1990; Fullan & Hargreaves, 1991; Fullan, 2001). When teachers are collegial and work in collaboration with administrators, positive school outcomes result. Researchers now consider the creation of a professional collaborative culture a critical component of successful schools.

Findings About Successful Schools

- Faculty in successful schools are less satisfied with regard to their teaching than are faculty in less successful schools.
- In successful schools, faculty members supervise and guide one another, plan courses together, and work in coordination.
- In successful schools, faculty members are not treated as subordinates, but instead are regarded as the colleagues of administrators and others involved in decisions and actions.
- Faculty members, administrators, and others in successful schools have established norms of collegiality for discussing and debating the big questions about how to constantly renew and improve the educational environment for all students.
- Successful schools seek, produce, and consume information, and they see educational renewal as a continuing process, not as an event.

SOURCE: Glickman, C. (1993). *Renewing America's schools* (pp. 16–18). San Francisco: Jossey-Bass.

In a professional collaborative culture, members of the school community work together effectively and are guided by a common purpose. All members of the community—teachers, administrators, students, and their families—share a common vision of what the school should be like. Together they create goals that lead them toward this vision. In doing so, they create a culture of discourse, where the most important educational matters facing the school are discussed openly and honestly. The teachers in these schools know they can be more effective and are continuously looking for the piece of advice, the book, the research, the organizational structure that will help them improve even more. The many different voices, experiences, and styles of the school community add to its strength and vitality.

Many studies, including the research Carl Glickman cites in his book *Renewing America's Schools,* support our view that a collaborative culture best builds and sustains effective teaching and learning in schools. Glickman reports that in successful schools, teachers are always questioning their practices; faculty members guide one another, plan together, coordinate their practices, and participate in the most important decisions; and the larger questions about educational practice are constantly at the forefront of meetings and conversations. These elements—faculty members working together, discussing important issues relevant to their role as professionals, and taking a significant role in the school's decision-making process—provide the foundation for developing a collaborative culture.

School governance structures engage the entire faculty—through teams, committees, and full faculty meetings—in deciding on key instructional, programmatic, and budgetary issues of the school. Many teachers are leaders, supported and nurtured by the principal. Teachers work in teams to plan and implement curricula and assessments for students they share and are members of groups such as Critical Friends Groups that train teachers to facilitate and engage in crucial conversations about instructional practice.

Benefits of Professional Collaboration for Teachers

Expectations for today's teachers are higher than ever before. Teachers are asked to prepare all students to reach high academic standards. In many schools, the complex learning needs of diverse student populations are presenting new challenges. Changing instructional methods and approaches and keeping up with current theories about teaching and learning require extensive intellectual preparation and training from teachers. Teachers can never know enough. Working together collaboratively enables teachers to pool their talents and resources for the benefit of all their students.

Benefits of Professional Collaboration for Students

Just as teachers are being called upon to stretch and expand their skills, so, too, are students expected to meet more complex challenges in their learning experiences. When Fred Newman and others studied over 10,000 students enrolled in 820 high schools across the United States, they found that when staff worked together collaboratively, students reaped the benefits (Newman & Wehlage, 1995). Students were more likely to be engaged in highly intellectual learning tasks; they achieved greater academic gains in math, science, history, and reading than students in traditionally organized schools; and a smaller achievement gap existed between students from different backgrounds than in the traditionally organized schools. (In smaller high schools, learning gains were distributed more equitably.)

Long-Term, Sustainable School Change

Building a culture of professional collaboration is critical for long-term, sustainable school change that results in improved student learning and achievement. When teachers work together and share decision making with administrators on key matters that affect the entire school, everyone stands to benefit. Working together effectively to solve problems and improve practice, teachers experience more job satisfaction and are able to create more authentic learning experiences for their students than when working in isolation. Students become more motivated, and their academic achievement increases.

Building a Collaborative Culture

To build a collaborative culture, all members of the school community must

- Share the belief that working collaboratively is the best way to reach the school's goals
- Develop organizational structures that allow teachers to form teams and work together
- Agree on norms so teams can work effectively
- Define a vision for the school based on competencies students should have
- Set goals to achieve the school vision

DEVELOPING A UNIFYING VISION

On a hot afternoon in September, a group of students, teachers, parents, community members, and administrators known as "The Butler Vision Team" sat around a school library table at Butler High School. Scattered across the table was a selection of student drawings, slips of paper, index cards, and meeting notes the group had collected over a one-month period. The Vision Team had asked members of the Butler School community to be part of creating the school's vision. In classrooms, at PTO meetings, in faculty meetings, and at community forums, the Vision Team asked people to look into a crystal ball and reflect upon what their ideal high school would look like, what they hoped students would be like when they left the school, and what they wished it were like to work and learn in the school.

One teacher asked, "I know our school's vision is important, but how are we ever going to compile all these papers into one succinct, clear message to guide our school?"

As members of the Vision Team started reading and talking about the papers, they found that most of the school community's various descriptions were similar in the picture they painted of what they wanted Butler High School to be.

Developing a vision (or mission) statement, clearly describing a school community's "dream school," is one of the most critical tasks a school undertakes on its road to becoming a small school. The process of creating this statement can be long and frustrating, causing many to scratch their heads and wonder, "How can such a short statement take so long to write? What's the big deal anyway?" Dealing with people's dreams, especially when they concern their children's futures, can be a complex and passionate undertaking. And yet, when developed correctly, the vision statement becomes a powerful tool, guiding many individuals on a common path for creating and sustaining school change.

The vision statement answers questions such as these:

- What should our school look like if we want to successfully educate all students?
- What are the students doing in this school?
- What do teaching and learning look and sound like?
- Are students painting, reading, doing experiments, dancing?
- Who's teaching them, and how?
- Are the classrooms noisy or quiet or both?
- How do people interact in our school?
- Are we finding ways for everyone to get a chance to participate and learn?

The Small Schools Principles and the School Vision

The Small School Principles play an important role in the development of a school vision. While these principles do not represent the "right answer" about what should be included in a vision statement, they do serve to remind us of the importance of articulating a vision that includes all students, provides opportunities for students to use their minds well, and promotes a professional, collaborative culture. Each school should have a unique vision that reflects both its individual identity and a deep understanding of the principles. Everybody should have a chance to provide input and be involved in creating a vision statement—teachers, students, parents, administrators, members of the community. Even before the statement is agreed upon and displayed on poster board in the school's front hall or sent home in the PTO newsletter, the process of reflecting and talking about what's important in a school can energize and unify the school community. Through discussion and exploration of differing interpretations on the part of individuals within the school community, the vision comes to life. The vision statement represents this process and becomes symbolic of a school's collaborative spirit. It sets the tone for future planning and development.

Celebrating the Vision

Once the entire school community has reached consensus on the wording of the school vision, it's time to celebrate! Some schools present the vision for the first time in a schoolwide assembly. Others publicize it in school newsletters and local papers. Copies of the vision can be posted in classrooms, the cafeteria, the gymnasium, the local grocery, and the public library. A flag with the vision statement can be paraded around the school. Whatever course a school decides to follow in presenting and celebrating the vision serves as an important affirmation of a school's commitment to improving all students' learning. With their displays of the vision, a school community makes a public statement about their intentions for the school.

Putting the Vision to Work

The vision statement focuses all the work of a school. It guides curriculum development, learning and teaching, and assessment. Planning teams revisit the statement when making key decisions about important issues such as curriculum, budgets, and student placement. Teacher teams look to the vision statement for guidance in solving problems. Often, when people start using the vision statement in real-school situations, they find certain parts of the statement need strengthening or rewording. The vision statement is a work-in-progress, revisited and fine-tuned as the school evolves.

The mission statement of Fenway High School in Boston reflects a deep commitment to social justice, equity, and activism. Each year the faculty goes on a retreat to review their mission statement and five-year plan to see how they're doing in support of this commitment. This year, faculty commented that although they continue to use essential questions that move students toward the school's mission (What does it mean to be human, and how do we learn the rules of life? How do you do the right thing in the face of injustice?), they weren't promoting as much activism as in past years. One teacher remarked, "We don't seem to be doing the letter-writing campaigns, the sit-ins, the political forums to the extent we did in the old days. We should take a look at trying to support kids to actually organize and do more politically motivated, anti-injustice activities in our city and community."

GOVERNING THE SCHOOL THROUGH SHARED LEADERSHIP AND TEACHER TEAMS

Small schools use leadership structures and decision-making procedures that model democratic practices. Guided by Principle 9, which calls for democratic forms of school governance and shared leadership, and in accordance with local and state requirements, small schools should have the autonomy to create their own governance structures for communication and decision making within the school. In small schools, the whole school community works together to set agendas and make decisions. A well-run school depends on ideas, experience, and input from every person involved.

Area of Autonomy 4

Governance and policies: Small schools should have the freedom to create their own governance structure that affords increased decision-making power over budget approval, principal selection and firing, and programs and policies, while being mindful of state requirements on school councils. This includes:

Having the school's site council take on increased governing responsibilities, including principal selection, supervision, and firing, with final approval by the superintendent in all cases; budget approval; and setting of school policies.

Giving the school freedom from all district policies and flexibility to set policies that the school community feels will best help students to be successful. This includes policies on such areas as promotion, graduation, attendance, and discipline.

Shared Leadership: Working Together Collaboratively

Small schools create governance structures such that all members of the school community—faculty and staff, parents and students, administrators, and community members—work together collaboratively and have a say in how the school is run. People representing the different stakeholders in the school community become active members of the major governing bodies of the school. Guided by a common purpose, these groups work together to set goals and make decisions that lead the school toward its vision. Members respect each other by valuing their differences and being open to each other's ideas. Even when there is disagreement, people listen to each other, because they believe deeply that differences and conflict are vital in the process of moving their school forward.

Shared leadership means that many people other than the administrators have both the information and the power to make decisions and enact changes. Instead of one or two people making decisions alone, working teams make decisions by consensus, with all participants voicing their opinions and either supporting or consenting to the change. Facilitative and shared leadership requires an operational structure that allows more people to lead the thinking of the school and to participate in making decisions at all levels. To build a practice of facilitative and shared leadership, a school forms teams and gives them significant responsibility, schedules regular meeting times, improves methods of communication, and finds effective ways to implement decisions.

With shared leadership, teachers become members of teams and play a substantial role in the change a school undertakes. As teachers participate in the school's Leadership Team, study groups, and academic and discipline-based teams, they are able to influence their school's direction and make decisions about the school's curriculum, teaching priorities, budget and expenditures, and hiring. When teachers have a genuine part in making decisions and implementing changes, they become more committed to reform efforts. In a collaborative culture, reform is not imposed upon teachers but created by them. Students' families and other community members also have a stake in the shared leadership of a school. Led by teams of teachers and the Leadership Team, the small school makes it possible for those outside of the school to participate in school reform. For example, the school might request feedback from parents on how to improve the family-school connection, or a parent might join a study group working on improving achievement for Black and Latino students. With these groups' new role in school leadership comes the responsibility to work closely with the school to understand its work and its needs.

The Changed Role of the Small School Principal

As small school principals move to share their authority by providing meaningful opportunities for teachers to participate in significant decision making, it is critical that they continually support teacher learning. In this new role, the principal recognizes that no one person in the building is the most knowledgeable or experienced practitioner. Rather, the principal is aware of the strengths of the staff and taps into each member's expertise to improve teaching and learning in the school. The principal works with the staff to develop a strong professional culture in which teachers collaborate continuously to ensure fulfillment of the school vision.

The Principal's Focus on Interconnected Areas

The principal's new role focuses on five interconnected areas.

- **Sharing real decision-making power with staff and faculty:** The principal shares authority by providing meaningful opportunities for teachers to participate in significant decision making. The principal works with the faculty to establish academic teams, discipline-based teams, study groups, and the Leadership Team, and communicates that every team's success is of paramount importance and that he or she will help them be successful.
- **Providing support for effective functioning of teams:** The principal ensures that teachers have the skills and understanding to participate effectively in teams. These skills include defining a purpose, creating norms for operating, setting agendas, and assigning tasks. The principal also gives ongoing feedback to teams, supporting and encouraging their work. Giving compliments and recognition to teams for their progress goes a long way toward supporting their work.
- **Being an instructional leader who prompts others to continuously learn and improve their practice:** As the instructional leader, the principal is often found in classrooms working with teachers and students, or in academic team meetings assisting in the development of effective teaching and learning strategies. In this role, the principal also procures instructional resources and professional development opportunities that improve learning, teaching, and assessment practices.
- **Developing collaborative accountability:** The principal works with the Leadership Team to hold individuals and teams accountable for reaching their goals. By asking teacher teams to document their progress, the principal and Leadership Team make it clear that every team's results matter, and that when a team reaches its goals, the whole school moves forward.
- **Managing and monitoring the change process to make sure it is always moving forward:** The principal and the Leadership Team ensure that all members of the school community clearly understand all parts of the change process and are committed to the vision.

Membership in School Governance Groups

- All major groups should be represented, with access always open to others.
- Regular classroom teachers should be in the majority.
- The school principal should be a "standing" (automatically included) member.
- The group as a whole should fairly represent the gender, ethnic, and economic populations of the entire school community.

Each school makes its own decisions about the kinds and number of collaborative governance teams they have. The following table gives examples of different kinds of teams, their membership, what they do, and recommendations for how often they should meet.

Table 7.2 Sample Groups Contributing to Shared Leadership and Decision Making in Small Schools

Name	Roles	Membership	Meetings
Design Team	Assists in initial planning and design of school.	Six to fifteen members, including educators from local school district, students, parents, and community members.	As needed
Governance Board	Has authority over (1) hiring and supervision of the principal (with the superintendent having final sign-off); (2) approval of the annual budget; and (3) setting of school policies (e.g., promotion and retention policies). Governance bodies have bylaws that detail what scope of decisions they make compared to those the principal and faculty make.	In Massachusetts, the Governance board is the school council, as defined by the Education Reform Act. High school councils consist of the principal, a number of parents equal to the number of professionals, community members, and at least one student. The principal and one other member are cochairs. The number of members is up to each school. Most states have guidelines for membership.	Once every four to eight weeks
Leadership Team	Coordinates change effort. Facilitates and manages data-based inquiry and decision making. Models shared leadership for the school. Develops collaborative accountability.	Six to twelve members, including teachers representing all student age levels and disciplines, the principal, instructional specialists, parents (optional), students (optional), and community members (optional).	Once every two weeks for two hours
Full Faculty	Makes decisions by consensus on all important, whole-school matters.	Full faculty.	Once a month

(Continued)

Table 7.2 (Continued)

Name	Roles	Membership	Meetings
Building Council (for small schools sharing a larger facility)	Coordinates and decides on use and scheduling for shared space within the building. Problem-solves plans for building renovations, etc.	Principals of each small school within a building.	Once a week
Academic Team	Develops instructional practice to improve teaching and learning for their students. Uses protocols for discussion and peer observation. Makes proposals to the Leadership Team for schoolwide changes in curriculum and instruction based on their work.	Two to six teachers who share the same students.	At lease twice a week for at least 45 minutes each time
Critical Friends Group	Primarily engaged in structured discussions about classroom practice. May develop proposals for full faculty to consider.	Six to ten teachers across grade levels and teams.	At least once a month for at least two hours
Study Group	Investigates a topic related to teaching and learning based on data and consensus from full faculty.	Four to eight members, mostly teachers; may include administrators, parents, and community members.	Every two to four weeks for one to two hours
Discipline-Based Team	Maps school curriculum within the discipline. Develops curriculum coherence within discipline from grade to grade. Identifies best practices within the discipline.	Staff who share the same content area; number varies by school.	At least once a month for at least two hours

A Study Group at Cass High School

Rushing out of the main office, tenth-grade teacher Harold Benson passed his colleague, Maria Cordero, in the hall.

"Hey, Maria, where does our study group meet this afternoon?" he asked.

"Tony's room. Did you get the article I put in your box?"

Looking over his shoulder, Harold called back, "Yeah, I liked that one a lot. Can't wait to hear what Tony has to say about it."

Harold Benson, Maria Cordero, Tony Maddux, and three other teachers from Cass High School are members of a study group investigating the effect of teacher expectations on low-performing students. After analyzing data revealing that 73 percent of students with an average of C– or lower reported that they have higher expectations for themselves than their teachers do, the faculty came to consensus that this was an important topic for a study group to investigate. The teachers formed a study group to better understand why students perceived that their teachers had low expectations of them and what could be done about it. They will use their findings to make recommendations to the full faculty and the Leadership Team.

Two months into the study, the teachers have read and discussed several articles on their topic. They have also interviewed twenty students—twelve students whose average is lower than a C– and eight students who have better than a B average. In the interviews, the students were asked to share their thoughts on how they and their teachers expect them to do in school.

At the study group's second presentation to the full faculty, Maria gave an update on their progress and preliminary findings. She also asked the faculty what questions they had about the topic and what directions the study group should take. The presentation and discussion that followed helped the faculty develop interest in the research and share their ideas. Eventually the whole school will look to this study group for guidance about how to improve the learning of students who have an average below C.

Focusing on Making Decisions With Educational Impact

Leadership Teams in effective schools focus their attention on those decisions that will have the greatest impact on improving student learning. They concentrate on "core" and "comprehensive" impact decisions, such as school budget, hiring, staff assignment, professional development, curriculum design, and student assessment.

"Zero" and "minimal" impact decisions, such as textbook adoption, attendance policy, lunchroom supervision, and parking, don't really change the fundamental teaching and learning practices in a school and should not be the focus of the Leadership Team. "Zero" and "minimal" impact decisions can be the work of subcommittees, study groups, or individual staff members.

It is helpful for schools to post guidelines for how each of these decisions is made (Glickman, 1993).

Working Together Effectively in Teams

Creating effective teacher teams that are committed to improving student, team, and school performance is a complex undertaking. Understanding what creates effective teams will help make teacher teams successful. Numerous studies and books chronicle the complexities of developing teams within organizations. These studies and books also document the practices that help teams meet their goals. Their findings can be adapted to schools.

Stages in Team Development

Bass and Avolio (1994) identify these five common stages that team members go through on their way to working together effectively:

1. **Forming:** The development of mutual acceptance during early meetings and activities. During this stage, team members are friendly and often will not disagree with each other's ideas.

2. **Storming:** The development of open, honest discussion of differences that can produce group conflicts. This stage is a natural part of developing trust and open dialogue about issues. Caring and honest acceptance of differences will foster better planning.

3. **Norming:** The team starts to establish the norms for working together, being productive, and cooperating. The team is meshing together and becoming more cohesive and creative as open and honest conflict gets resolved into productive working relationships.

4. **Performing:** The team has its goals, working roles, and norms; members can solve problems openly and honestly, plan new programs, and communicate with each other and the rest of the staff.

5. **Reforming:** All teams eventually lose and then add members. In this stage, the team begins anew as old members move on and new members are added. The process of becoming a team starts again.

Characteristics of Effective Teams

A detailed discussion of each of these characteristics of effective teams follows this list. In schools, effective teams

- Have a culture of discourse at their center
- Have a clearly defined purpose that guides their work, and specific, measurable goals that they achieve

- Are committed to norms that guide how the team operates
- Are disciplined in maintaining their focus
- Communicate effectively within the team and with those outside of the team
- Improve the ability of team members to function as a team in the future

Discourse: Effective teams have a culture of discourse at their center.

In a culture of discourse, team members discuss and think about significant issues related to improving teaching, learning, and assessment. Team members demonstrate respect for each other by valuing differences of opinion and being open-minded in regard to others' ideas. Disagreements and challenges are welcomed in team discussions, as they often push collective thinking to a deeper level. Ultimately, many of these conversations result in improved student learning and growth.

It takes time and discipline to raise the quality of teacher discourse—focusing on ideas and application rather than on the housekeeping details that often take up so much of teachers' time. Teams may use text-based discussions, case studies, and protocols for looking at student work to deepen their conversations and get them focused on the substantial issues surrounding teaching and learning. At times, meetings can become uncomfortable when a group is hashing out important and difficult issues. However, when a culture of discourse is at the center of a team's operations, the work of the team is better informed by the expertise of its members and more likely to effect lasting change.

Purpose: Effective teams have a clearly defined purpose that guides their work, and specific, measurable goals that they achieve.

The most successful teams have a purpose or mission they are deeply committed to that drives them forward. A clearly defined purpose energizes a team because all members understand exactly why they are together. Similar to an overarching goal, the purpose or mission defines the general intent of the team. The common purpose serves to keep the team focused at all times. All actions and decisions must make sense relative to this purpose.

Specific, measurable goals are the steps that will lead a team toward accomplishing its purpose and making an impact on the school or students. Too often in schools, committees continue to meet and plan, but fail to achieve measurable results. Often, at the end of the school year, or when the team loses its momentum, little or no action has taken place. Clear, measurable goals prevent this wheel-spinning by focusing discussion on action and how to achieve the desired outcomes.

Norms: Effective teams define and are committed to norms that guide how the team operates.

Norms are ways of working together that can help groups be more thoughtful and productive. Norms exist in every learning community, whether or not they are named or agreed upon. In the process of formally establishing productive norms, a group identifies the ways it wants to be and work together for the purpose of achieving and being held accountable for its goals. In such an environment, people voice, question, support, disagree, and take risks, while working together respectfully and purposefully toward shared goals.

As groups of teachers work together, the variety of approaches they represent may lead to unproductive conflict and disagreement if there are no ground rules for conversation and planning. Setting norms of mutual respect and equal participation, for example, can help groups deal with the common disagreements and conflicts that often stall or derail effective group work. Group members agree to norms in the areas of logistics, timeliness, courtesy, decision making, workload assignments, and priority setting, because they are guided by the common purpose of improving their school.

Focus: Effective teams are disciplined in maintaining their focus.

Teams in small schools have numerous responsibilities. How a team manages these differing roles and relationships affects their success. The successful team uses its purpose, goals, and norms to maintain its focus. With each new idea, discussion, or possibility, all team members should ask whether the issue fits the purpose, moves them toward achieving the performance goals, and can be dealt with within the team's operating approach.

To maintain focus, team members should continuously assess the team's work. Keeping records of lessons learned, ideas discussed, decisions made, actions taken, and communication with people outside the team can help in evaluating a team's focus.

Communication: Effective teams communicate within the team and with those outside the team.

Depending on the nature of their work, teams must communicate with other teachers, the Leadership Team, the principal, other teams, parents, students, or the larger community outside of school. Effective communication informs other members of the school community of a team's progress and allows outside groups to aid the team's work. Teams need clear systems for passing on materials, discussions, and results from their work. Distributing minutes or short updates to those affected by or connected to the work helps keep those outside the team informed. Giving presentations to other teams or parent groups, creating team portfolios, or inviting community members to sit in on meetings are other ways for teacher teams to build bridges to those who can help them.

Progress: Effective teams improve the ability of their members to function as a team in the future.

While it is important that a team reach its goals, how they reach them is equally important. Truly dynamic teams show evidence of growth over time. For example, in the first year, members may become familiar with the team format and protocols used to guide discussions. In subsequent years, teams may make individual refinements and changes according to their needs. With experience, team members learn to work together better while they develop skills that they can bring to other teams they may work with in the future. Improving each member's capacity for teamwork not only helps the existing team, but moves the whole school forward. These team skills may include developing trust among group members, being open and honest with feedback and praise, creating agendas, developing communication methods, and facilitating meetings.

TOOLS FOR BUILDING A CULTURE OF ADULT LEARNERS

Assessing Your School's Culture

Tool 7.1: Building a Collaborative School Culture: How Are We Doing?

Purpose: To assess current school culture in order to discuss areas for improvement.

Directions: For the following questions, rate how you think your school is doing. Then discuss areas of weakness and ways to improve. Use this scale:

1 = No, or rarely, or only a few teachers

2 = Some, but not much, or not everyone

3 = Most teachers and teams do fairly regularly

4 = All teachers do regularly

Do we:

_____ Discuss student work in teams using defined protocols and use these discussions to take steps to improve learning, teaching, and assessment?

_____ Observe classrooms and have follow-up conversations with the teacher to improve learning, teaching, and assessment?

_____ Work in teacher teams to plan and implement curricula and assessments for shared students?

_____ Engage in text-based discussions?

_____ Use Critical Friends Groups to bring instructional dilemmas to the forefront and receive feedback on them?

_____ Work in study groups to examine data, conduct action research, and try new strategies for improving learning, teaching, and assessment?

_____ Serve on faculty panels to judge and assess student work that is presented through exhibitions, demonstrations, and portfolios?

_____ Work in teacher teams to develop rubrics for assessing student work?

_____ Collaboratively examine multiple sources of data to identify challenges, and then use an inquiry process to develop schoolwide solutions?

Have we:

_____ Set norms as a faculty for how we work with each other?

_____ Developed a shared vision and common agenda among the entire school community for moving the school forward?

_____ Developed schoolwide habits of mind?

_____ Created a shared decision-making governance structure that engages the entire faculty through teams, committees, and full faculty meetings to decide on key instructional, programmatic, and budgetary issues of the school?

Tool 7.2: Survey on Findings of Successful Schools

Purpose: To analyze the current state of collaborative work in your school in relation to five findings of successful schools (Glickman, 1993, pp.17–18).

Directions: For the following findings, rate how you think your school is doing. Then come together as a group for sharing. Discuss areas of weakness and suggest ways to improve. Use this scale:

1 = This finding does not characterize our school at all.

2 = There is little evidence of this finding in our school.

3 = There is some evidence of this finding in our school.

4 = This finding characterizes what goes on in our school.

_____ "Faculty in successful schools are less satisfied with regard to their teaching than are faculty in the less successful schools."

_____ "Successful schools are places where faculty members supervise and guide one another, plan courses together, and work in coordination."

_____ "In successful schools, faculty members are not treated as subordinates, but instead are regarded as the colleagues of administrators and others involved in decisions and actions."

_____ "Faculty members, administrators, and others in successful schools have established norms of collegiality for discussing and debating the big questions about how to constantly renew and improve the educational environment for all students."

_____ "Successful schools seek, produce, and consume information, and they see educational renewal as a continuing process, not as an event."

Developing a Unifying Vision Statement

Tool 7.3: Powerful Learning Experience

Purpose: To show the relationship between an individual's powerful learning experience and principles of effective learning and teaching.

Directions: You will need paper for the writing activity, flip charts to record discussion, and copies of the CCE principles of effective teaching and learning.

1. **Guided writing activity:** Individuals take time to reflect on and then write about a powerful learning experience that they have had either inside or outside of school. A powerful learning experience is one where you experience a feeling of "aha!" It can be an individual or group learning experience where the learning is personal and meaningful, with positive and lasting outcomes. (5–10 minutes)

2. **Discussion in pairs:** In pairs, share and discuss the powerful learning experience you wrote about. List characteristics of your experiences. (5 minutes)

3. **Group discussion:** As someone facilitates a group discussion about the powerful learning experiences, someone else records characteristics on chart paper. A list of common characteristics of the powerful learning experiences discussed is compiled to summarize the discussion. (10–15 minutes)

4. **Principles of effective learning and teaching:** Make copies of the CCE principles of effective teaching and learning and hand them out. In pairs, see where the characteristics of the group's powerful learning experiences are reflected in these principles. (5–10 minutes)

5. **Group discussion:** Facilitate a discussion about the common characteristics and where they are reflected in the ten principles. Discuss ways of incorporating them in the school vision statement. (5–10 minutes)

Tool 7.4: Developing a Vision Statement

Purpose: To develop a vision statement that is consistent with principles for effective learning and teaching.

Directions:

1. *Form a "Vision Team" to facilitate the process.* Members should include students, parents, faculty, staff, administration, and people from the community.

2. *Gather ideas from students, parents, faculty, and others.* Ask small groups in classrooms and at special meetings to reflect on what they think their school should be like by responding to questions such as these:
   - What does my ideal school look like?
   - What does learning and teaching look like in my ideal school?
   - What do we want all students to know and be able to do by the time they leave this school?
   - How do people interact in my ideal school?

Students may provide written responses as an essay assignment or as a culmination of class discussions. Parents and other community members provide input through a simple survey or in focus-group activities.

3. *Draft the vision.* The vision team synthesizes the views and ideas presented in step 2 above and writes a draft vision. Use the checklist at the end of this outline to make sure the draft reflects principles for effective learning and teaching.

4. *Review and redraft the statement.* Circulate the draft among members of the school community for comment and consensus. The Vision Team then makes any necessary changes.

5. *Approve the vision.* Present the vision at a meeting of the full faculty for approval and adoption.

6. *Display, celebrate, and keep the vision alive.* The whole school community affirms, displays, and celebrates the vision. Hold a public celebration of the vision that involves everyone. Display the vision in all rooms and use it as a basis for decision making in the school.

Vision Statement Checklist

Answering the questions on this checklist will help you make sure your school's vision statement is in line with principles of effective learning and teaching. This checklist may be used during the entire vision development process and especially during the review and redrafting stages.

_____ Was the vision developed collaboratively?

_____ How does the statement promote equity?

_____ How is it useful as a tool to develop curriculum and assessment?

_____ Is the language clear and succinct?

_____ Where are principles of effective teaching and learning embedded?

_____ How does the vision seek to improve academic achievement and learning for all students?

_____ How do we communicate the vision to all members of the school community?

_____ How do we celebrate and make it public to the whole school community?

_____ How often do we plan to revisit it?

_____ How can we tell if the vision is embedded in all the work of the school?

SOURCE: Future Protocol "Back from the Future," by Scott Murphy. Used with permission of the National School Reform Faculty (NSRF), Harmony Education Center, Bloomington, IN (http://www.nsrfharmony.org).

Working Effectively in Teams

Tool 7.5: Setting Norms for Collaborative Work

Purpose: To become familiar with different areas to consider when setting norms and to set norms for collaborative work.

Directions: Have groups read the following before doing the norm-setting activity:

What are norms? Norms are ways of working together that can help groups be more thoughtful and productive. They fall into two categories: procedural and interpersonal. Once norms have been established, it is important that the entire group, not just the facilitator, takes responsibility for making sure that the norms are respected and for redirecting the group when they are not. Norms can change and evolve as the group develops and matures.

Operating as a team. Norms need to be set in many different areas, including decision making, logistics, how to give feedback, how to treat each other, how the norms will be monitored, and the roles team members will take. Within each area, the essential question is, "How do we want to operate as a team?" Following are some key components:

- *Logistics:* These are the nuts and bolts of how the team operates. Examples of logistical issues include meeting schedule, start time, end time, lateness policy, and attendance. Although they seem like small matters, many of these items can become much larger issues unless they are spelled out clearly and accepted by all team members.
- *Courtesy:* People have different styles of participating and different levels of tolerance for discussion, disagreement, and interruption. The norms set in these areas are designed to help team members communicate with each other in a respectful and caring fashion. Setting norms for how to listen, participate, and handle conflict allows team members to discuss and decide how they want to treat each other.
- *Decision-making process:* How will the team make decisions? Reach agreements? How will the team show agreement? Any significant decisions that affect the entire team should be decided by consensus, because this method is most effective for incorporating differing viewpoints and for creating the discourse that contributes to a collaborative culture. Consensus requires that all members express opinions on any decision and agree that they can live with the decision that is being considered. Any decision a team makes should be judged on two criteria: (1) how well the decision deals with the matters at hand, and (2) how committed the group members are to carrying it out.
- *Workload assignment:* How will work be assigned? How will conflicts with existing workloads be settled?
- *Setting priorities:* How will the team discharge responsibility for on-time completion and equal distribution?
- *Enforcement of norms:* How will the team make sure the norms are followed?

Sample Ways to Express Opinions

Thumbs up: I'm in favor of the decision.

Thumbs down: I don't agree with the decision.

Thumbs in neutral: I'm not 100% behind the decision, but I can live with it.

To reach consensus, there should be no thumbs down. In order to build consensus, sometimes groups table decisions to allow time to get more data and information and take a vote at a subsequent meeting.

ACTIVITY FOR SETTING NORMS/SETTING COMMUNITY AGREEMENTS

In this activity, members of a team write statements about how they want their team to operate, and then categorize the statements into procedural norms and interpersonal norms. The group discusses the statements and reaches consensus on norms for their group.

Directions

The facilitator passes out sticky notes to each team member.

Each person writes a norm, or a statement about how he or she wants the group to work together, on a sticky note.

The team shares its individual notes and divides them into the two categories—procedural norms and interpersonal norms.

Within each category, group the suggestions that are similar (for example, *take turns speaking* and *make sure everyone speaks* should be grouped together).

Give a name to the norm for each group. (From the example above, the norm could be "Make sure everyone is heard.")

The group discusses the norms that have been suggested and checks to see whether or not the group is in agreement. The group should reach consensus on the ones it accepts.

Notes

The team will work with greater commitment if they themselves generate their norms.

Post the norms during each meeting.

Reflect on norms at the end of each meeting.

Add new norms as the team develops and new situations arise.

Tool 7.6: Understanding Governance in Small Schools

Purpose: To gain an understanding of *Area of Autonomy 4: Governance and policies*, and to begin to chart out who makes which decisions at the new small school.

Directions

1. Introduce participants and workshop goals:
   - To gain an understanding of *Area of Autonomy 4: Governance and policies*
   - To begin to chart out who makes which decisions at the new small school
   - To begin a dialogue about the challenges, supports, and resources needed to implement this autonomy
   - To begin writing a draft on the new small school governance structure

2. Present *Area of Autonomy 4: Governance and policies*
   - Have triads record questions about the autonomy and how it will work in their school.
   - Chart questions one at a time. Synthesize and group into categories.

3. The Who and What of decision making
   - Ask, "In your new small school, which bodies should make what decisions?"
   - Have one group write different kinds of school decisions on sticky notes and place these on chart paper.
   - Have another group record on sticky notes which different groups they believe should be active in school decision making, and place these on another piece of chart paper.
   - Have the large group match the decisions and decision-maker sticky notes on a third piece of chart paper.
   - Share with the whole group.

4. Challenges, strategies, and supports
   - Have groups chart challenges they anticipate in making decisions more collaboratively, strategies to help overcome these challenges, and supports and resources they will need.
   - Share with the full group.

5. Next Steps and Reflection (15 minutes)

Tool 7.7: Governance Structure Chart

Purpose: To discuss and record who should have decision-making responsibility in different areas of school operation.

Directions: Use this chart to record who should have decision-making authority and who should have input and/or recommendations. Each school may adapt the categories to fit its particular context. The goal of this chart is to create a democratic governance structure of shared decision making.

Key: *D = Decision-making authority:* makes the final decision; *I = Gives input:* has a formal opportunity to give input and/or recommendations for a pending decision.

Table 7.3

Category	Students	Families	Teachers	Full Admin Team	Principal	Leadership Team	Governing Board	Faculty Teams
Vision/mission								
School vision/mission	I	I	I	I	I	I	D	I
Strategic plan								
Teaching and Learning								
Curriculum								
Student assessment								
Professional development								
Student Support								
Counseling								
Advisories								
Guidance								
Operations								
Budget								
Hiring staff								
Hiring principal								
Staffing patterns								
Facilities								
Student enrollment								
Fundraising								
School resources								

(Continued)

Table 7.3 (Continued)

Category	Students	Families	Teachers	Full Admin Team	Principal	Leadership Team	Governing Board	Faculty Teams
Organization								
Schedule								
Student policies								
Code of conduct								
Family and community engagement								
Evaluation								
Staff								
Administrators								
Principal								
School								
Other Categories:								

Tool 7.8: Guidelines for Effective Meetings

Purpose: To provide a list of guidelines for running effective meetings.

Directions: When a team is first established, it is helpful to distribute the following guidelines for discussion. You may adapt them to fit the needs of individual teams and revisit these guidelines as necessary.

Guidelines
- The agenda is distributed with sufficient time for members to prepare for the meeting.
- Members arrive on time for meetings.
- Meetings start and end at the scheduled times.
- Each meeting has an assigned facilitator, recorder, and timekeeper. (Often these are rotating positions.)
- Teams follow norms they have established together. These may include
  - trusting that members can say what they truly feel about an issue;
  - keeping confidentiality when members agree to do so;
  - asking clarifying questions when in doubt about an issue;
  - having a chance to consider more than one solution to an issue;
  - thoroughly understanding an issue before reaching consensus;
  - encouraging participation by everyone, even the quietest members.

- There are set time limits for the meeting (and for individual agenda items when possible).
- At the end of each meeting, the facilitator summarizes what has been accomplished. Plans regarding "who will do what by when" are finalized and recorded in the minutes.
- The recorder distributes minutes of meetings to all team members in a timely fashion.
- Someone takes responsibility for communicating regularly with the Leadership Team and other interested groups. (This may be a rotating position.)
- Periodically, teams evaluate meeting efficiency, productivity, and use of time.

Tool 7.9: Sample Format for Recording Team Meetings

Purpose: To provide a form for team meeting records.

Directions: This form may be reproduced for recording several agenda items at a meeting.

Team:	Date:	
Members Present:		
Agenda item:	Time allotment:	
Discussion notes:		
Action plan:	People responsible:	Deadline:
Agenda item:	Time allotment:	
Discussion notes:		
Action plan:	People responsible:	Deadline:

Tool 7.10: Compass Points: An Exercise
in Understanding Preferences in Group Work

Purpose: To enable teams to explore various preferences that individual members have in approaching team work, to enlarge understanding of the strengths and limitations of each preference, and to suggest ways to utilize these differences in a team's work.

Overview: The activity includes
- Identifying one's style of work within a group
- Working with others of the same style to identify a particular style's strengths and limitations for members whose styles are different
- Sharing strengths and limitations with members who have other styles
- Developing a common group value for all compass point styles
- Validating everyone's contributions while recognizing one's limitations

Participants: Compass Points works best with a group of 15–40 members. If the group is smaller, some parts of the activity (group discussion and debriefing) need to be adjusted. If the group is larger, more time should be allotted to the discussions and debriefing.

Directions

1. Make copies and pass out the Personal Work Styles sheet at the end of this tool. Have members circle individually which direction they believe accurately describes the way they work within a group. (It is important to make this distinction, because we often work differently within a group than we do on our own.) Have members do this without any discussion.

2. After individuals have identified themselves privately on paper (1–5 minutes), separate the group into four smaller groups by direction: North, South, East, or West.
   - Have groups answer Work Style Questions on the sheet that follows this tool. Chart their responses, and be prepared to report back to the full group.
   - Do not give any more directions than the last sentence. The manner in which each group proceeds with the task is very telling about their styles of work.
   - Give groups a 15- to 30-minute time limit. Be firm about the time limits, since the way that groups deal with time limits is also very telling.
   - Give groups a large sheet of chart paper to record their answers.
   - Do not give groups any direction or requirements about the way their answers should be recorded or about the way they should report back to the full group. The styles that groups use even to make a wall chart are telling.

3. If the activity is being conducted by a leader or group of leaders who have previously done Compass Points, it can be interesting and useful to have the leaders sit in with the four groups, strictly as observers. It is often valuable for a leader to sit in on a group that does not match his or her personal style. For example, if you see yourself as an East, sit in as an observer with the Norths, etc. Don't give any comments or let your facial expressions give away what you observe.

4. When the time is up, reconvene as a large group and post the charts. The leaders can suggest that everyone take a look at the ways different groups completed the task.

5. Have direction groups take turns sharing their responses with the full group. Members can feel free to ask questions or make some remarks, but this time should be used mostly to listen and learn, not to discuss relative merits of the styles. If leaders or others served as group observers, it can be valuable to have them share their observations on the manner in which different groups approached their task.

6. When groups have finished, the leader or leaders can facilitate the group in a debriefing of the activity. The following questions can be useful in providing insights for the entire group.
   - Did individuals believe they were in the right direction group?
   - How could they tell?
   - What ratio of the different compass points would make an effective and productive team?
   - What would happen if a team were missing one of the directions?
   - What would happen if a team were made up of only one direction?
   - How can knowing this information be useful in your work as a team?
   - How can a team balance having fun, getting work done, and allowing for personal styles?

COMPASS POINTS: PERSONAL WORK STYLES

Directions: Circle which "direction" you think best describes the way you work within a group.

Personal Work Styles

NORTH: Acting–"Let's do it!"

Likes to act, try things, plunge in.

EAST: Speculating

Likes to look at the big picture and possibilities before taking action.

SOUTH: Caring

Likes to know that everyone's feelings have been taken into consideration and that all voices have been heard before taking action.

WEST: Paying attention to detail

Likes to know the who, what, when, where, and why before taking action.

COMPASS POINTS: PERSONAL STYLE QUESTIONS

Directions: Record each group's answers on this form or on chart paper.

What are the strengths of our style? (list four adjectives)

What are the limitations of our style? (list four adjectives)

What style do we find the most difficult to work with? Why?

What do others need to know about us that will make our work together more successful?

SOURCE: Used with permission of the National School Reform Faculty (NSRF), Harmony Education Center, Bloomington, IN (http://www.nsrfharmony.org).

<hr>

Tool 7.11: Text-Based Seminar

Purpose: To enable a team to examine a relevant issue in depth by focusing on a short article or excerpt from a book.

Directions: In a text-based seminar of forty minutes to one hour, a team examines an issue from an outside point of view by focusing on a specific article or excerpt from a book. This seminar helps build a culture of discourse in a school by allowing for enlargement of intellectual understanding. Participants read a short article or excerpt from a book that is related to teaching and learning and then engage in a discussion about the text. The purpose of the discussion is not to persuade other group members of a particular point of view, but to clarify, build upon, and enhance understanding of the text. Text-based seminars give participants an opportunity to extract different meanings and ideas from a text and to discuss important issues related to the text.

1. *Select the text:* Choose an article or book excerpt that will have implications for teaching and learning. The article may be selected by the team facilitator or by an individual member of the team.

2. *Read the text:* If the text is long, the facilitator may distribute it before the meeting, or a shorter text may be read for the first time during the meeting. If participants have already read the text, allow five minutes of seminar time to review it. If a short article is to be read during the seminar, ten to fifteen minutes should be enough. While reading, participants may take notes, underline or highlight important ideas, and record questions the text raises for them.

3. *Begin the discourse:* There are two effective ways to begin the discourse. Each member of the seminar may take turns reading aloud a sentence or two that has particular significance to them, and share why they responded to that particular excerpt. Alternately, the facilitator may present a framing question to start the discussion.

4. *Discuss the text:* The facilitator leads a twenty- to thirty-minute discussion. He or she should remind participants to refer to the text to support their comments. Groups may want to follow these guidelines:

   Listen actively.

   Build on what others say.

   Expose/suspend your assumptions.

   Don't step on others' talk. Silences and pauses are OK.

   Emphasize clarification, amplification, and implications of ideas.

   Converse directly with each other, not through the facilitator.

   Let the conversation flow without raising hands, as much as possible.

   Make references to the text and encourage others to do the same.

   Watch your "airtime" for how often you speak and how much you say when you speak.

5. *Close the discussion:* The facilitator closes the discussion about the text, highlighting two or three main points of discussion and thanking participants for their perspectives. The result is that all participants leave the seminar with a deeper understanding of the text. Many times this leads to agreement for further exploration of the topic.

<hr>

SOURCE: Gene Thompson-Grove, "Text-Based Seminar Guidelines." Used with permission of the National School Reform Faculty (NSRF), Harmony Education Center, Bloomington, IN (http://www.nsrfharmony.org).

Tool 7.12: The Final Word

Purpose: To expand a group's understanding of a text or texts in a focused way and in a limited amount of time.

Directions: Have groups read through a selected text or texts before the meeting. In preparation, each person should select and mark one significant quote or section from the text(s). During the rounds described below, participants will discuss these quotes or sections. Working in groups of four with a designated timekeeper/facilitator, have four rounds of discussion (15 minutes each).

Procedure for each round

1. Begin by designating a facilitator/timekeeper. This role should not be filled by the person who will begin the round (and who has the FINAL WORD).

2. One person begins by explaining the significance of her or his quote/section from the text(s) to the group. (4 minutes)

3. After this person is finished, each person then comments on the same quote/section. You may choose to respond to what the first person has said, or to speak to the quote or section in any other way that extends the group's understanding of the text. Each person in the group has three minutes to respond, for a total of nine minutes.

4. The person who started then has the FINAL WORD. (2 minutes)
   • Each round begins with a different person explaining to the group the significance of her or his quote/selection from the text(s).

SOURCE: Daniel Baron. Used with permission of the National School Reform Faculty (NSRF), Harmony Education Center, Bloomington, IN (http://www.nsrfharmony.org).

Tool 7.13: The Obstacle Resolution Protocol

Purpose: To resolve an obstacle in progress toward a desired outcome.

Directions: Before the meeting, each person in the group reflects on ONE obstacle that is keeping her/him from making progress toward a desired outcome. While there may be many obstacles, this protocol focuses on one at a time. Additional sessions may be scheduled to deal with multiple obstacles. Work in groups of four, with a designated timekeeper/facilitator for each of the four rounds.

Procedure for each round

1. Begin by designating a facilitator/timekeeper. This role should not be filled by the person who will begin the round (and who will resolve his or her obstacle).

2. One person begins by explaining the obstacle he or she is facing and any related context. (4 minutes)

3. After this person is finished, each person then comments on the obstacle and offers alternatives for overcoming the obstacle. The premise here is that after all obstacles have been resolved, the underlying goal can be achieved. Each person in the group has three minutes to respond, for a total of nine minutes.

4. The person who started will then discuss how he or she intends to resolve the obstacle. (2 minutes)
   - Each round beings with a different person explaining his or her obstacle.

Tool 7.14: Making Decisions by Consensus

Purpose: To provide guidelines for reaching decisions by consensus.

Directions: Consensus means general agreement. For consensus to exist, it is not necessary for every member to agree in full, but for every participant to have a chance to be heard and, in the end, be able to "live with" the final decision. Participants don't have to consider the decision made to be the best one, but the decision should not violate any member's personal convictions. There should be no member who strongly opposes the group's decision.

Reaching consensus requires
- time
- active participation from all members
- skills in communication, active listening, conflict resolution, and facilitation
- creative thinking and open-mindedness

When facilitating for consensus
- Help the group work together in positive ways.
- Clearly state the problem and ask the group to arrive at a solution that they all can live with.
- Take disagreement for granted, but do not emphasize it.
- Involve everyone in the discussion.
- Use brainstorming as a tool to generate many ideas without judgment.
- Consider all ideas, one by one, giving pros and cons and modifying the ideas when necessary.
- Identify two to three of the best, most workable solutions.
- When necessary, remind the group of its goal—to reach consensus.
- Ask the group to show a "thumbs up" if they agree with or can live with the decision, and a "thumbs down" if they cannot.

Consensus checklist
_____ Did each member give an opinion?

_____ Did each idea presented receive comments and consideration?

_____ Did members who disagreed with the decision express their concerns, reservations, and feelings before the idea was adopted?

_____ Is any team member hesitant to actively support the decision?

Tool 7.15: Assessing a Team's Quality of Work

Purpose: To provide areas of discussion and sample indicators for teams to use to assess their work.

Directions: To maintain the quality and effectiveness of a team's work, team members need to take time to reflect on what the team is doing. Following are areas of discussion that can help teams assess their work. Teams may use these questions to gauge their work and use the indicator chart for each question to note the team's effectiveness.

1. How effective is our team in developing practices that improve student learning?

Not effective	Very effective

Sample indicators

- What practices for instructing and assessing our students have we changed, tried, or added to our repertoire?
- How have we addressed the needs of diverse learners?
- Do we use protocols for looking at student work to tell us how our students are doing?
- Do we observe each other's classrooms and have follow-up discussions about what we observe to improve learning, teaching, and assessment?
- Have we developed rubrics or assessment criteria for assessing student work?

2. How effective are we in communicating our work?

Not effective	Very effective

Sample indicators

- Do we allow time at each team meeting for an update from the Leadership Team liaison?
- Do we maintain and distribute clear, concise minutes to team members and others who may be interested?
- Do we employ multiple ways of communicating our work, such as newsletters, email communication, displays, presentations to other groups, and a team mailbox?

- Do we allow time for team members to socialize?
- Do we include written reflections on our team's work and progress as part of team meetings?

3. How effective are we in team facilitation and decision making?

Not effective	Very effective

Sample indicators

- Have we established team norms and do we respect them?
- Do we make team decisions by consensus?
- Do we use the expertise of individual teachers and teams to inform our thinking on specific issues?
- Do we make presentations to the full faculty for decisions on issues that impact the entire school?
- Do we make sure every team member is accountable for team progress and performances?

The Practice of a Collaborative Culture

When one of the ninth-grade teams at West High School first started meeting to look at and discuss student work, Ms. Wilkes, an English teacher, was reluctant to participate. She felt she had enough work of her own to do correcting papers, planning lessons, and meeting with parents after school. With all she had on her plate, giving up an hour of time to sit around talking about other kids' work just didn't seem worth it.

Besides, the idea of laying her and her students' work on the table for others to critique made her feel vulnerable. Even the norms the group had established of listening thoughtfully and openly and treating others and their work with respect and support didn't reassure her.

After several sessions of using protocols to discuss the work of her colleagues, however, Ms. Wilkes began to gain confidence in the process. Together, the team had helped the science teacher fine-tune her lab writing assignments so that the students' lab reports were more focused. They helped the social studies teacher rephrase an assignment he gave every year to encourage students to not only recount but interpret historical events.

Four months after they first started meeting, Ms. Wilkes decided to go for it. She brought in a sampling of persuasive essays her students had written. She was frustrated with the haphazard organization of the essays and didn't know what to do. Her question for the group was this: How can I get my students to develop their arguments in a more deliberate way?

After much discussion, Ms. Wilkes realized that she needed to allow her students more time for writing workshops before they started the essays and more peer editing between drafts.

AUTHOR'S NOTE: Portions of this chapter were previously published in CCE's Turning Points guides, *Looking Collaboratively at Student and Teacher Work* (2001), *Guide to Data-Based Inquiry and Decision Making* (2001), and *Guide to Collaborative Culture and Shared Leadership* (2001).

In professional collaborative cultures, teachers engage in a number of practices with the goal of improving student learning. Colleagues use protocols to look at student and teacher work, offering support and feedback. Failure, mistakes, and uncertainty are openly shared and discussed, often leading to greater risk taking and experimentation in instructional practice. Text-based seminars encourage participants to read and discuss texts using a text-based discussion protocol. Instructional and curriculum dilemmas are presented and solved in consultancies. By combining peer observations in classrooms with conversations about the observations, teachers find ways to improve learning, teaching, and assessment. And with the practice of data-based inquiry and decision making, teachers examine multiple sources of data to identify challenges and use an inquiry process to develop schoolwide solutions.

USING PROTOCOLS TO LOOK AT STUDENT AND TEACHER WORK

The practice of looking collaboratively at student and teacher work results in teachers' making refinements to instruction, curriculum, and assessment with the goal of improving student learning. Schools collect data to document how close students are to meeting the school's learning goals. Since student work is one of the most authentic data sources teachers have to gauge student progress, teachers engage in a structured process to analyze and discuss this work. This process, in which teachers meet in small groups led by a facilitator, is called a protocol.

During a protocol, groups made up primarily of teachers—but also including administrators, parents, students, and members of the community—meet regularly for a specific period of time to share and discuss student work. This work is usually in response to teacher assignments in class or for homework and includes essays, drawings, projects, presentations, portfolios, and videos. The purpose of these conversations is to examine the work in order to arrive at a more formal understanding of learning, teaching, and assessment. To make sure the focus of each conversation stays on improving student learning, groups use protocols that provide structure and guidelines for their discussion. This is not a time to make judgments about student or teacher work, but to collectively seek ways to improve it.

The school schedule reflects this commitment to improving student learning by allowing for regularly scheduled, significant amounts of time for protocols. Looking collaboratively at student work requires more teacher time than does individually grading the work. Finding time for this in-depth process can be a challenge. However, the benefits to the school community at large indicate the importance of creating the time and space.

Benefits of Looking at Student and Teacher Work

There are many benefits of looking at student and teacher work. They include:

- **Gaining a more comprehensive understanding of student competencies.** Student work helps teachers get inside students' heads and understand what they are thinking and how their thinking is developing over time.
- **Embedding professional development in teachers' daily practices to improve student achievement.** When teachers participate in ongoing conversations about teaching and learning, they promote the practice of reflective thinking about their beliefs, assumptions, and practices. Collegial feedback and critical analysis of student and teacher work in a safe and structured format create a culture of continuous learning. Looking at student work can be one way to strengthen connections between student learning and changes in instruction, curriculum, and other aspects of school life.
- **Building a sense of community.** Looking collaboratively at student work and participating in collective problem solving moves teachers away from the isolating concept of "my students" and toward the community concept of "our students." These practices develop a culture of shared problem solving and demonstrate the power of focusing multiple perspectives on a single issue.
- **Fostering a culture that collaboratively assesses the quality and challenge of teacher assignments.** Collegial feedback and discussion enable teachers to critically analyze whether their assignments or units ask students to construct knowledge, develop habits of mind, and make connections between school and the real world.
- **Developing shared, public criteria to assess student work.** As teachers look at student and teacher work, they develop a shared language for assessing the work and a common understanding of what quality student work looks like. When these criteria are made public and shared with students, the quality of their work continues to improve. When looking at and discussing student work, the development, consideration, and negotiation of standards at all levels—personal, local, community, and national—must be important elements in the conversation.

What Goes on During a Protocol?

There are different protocols for different purposes, but in general each protocol follows a similar pattern, with these five parts: presentation of student work by the presenter; questions to the presenter from the group about the presentation; group feedback about the work; response to feedback from the presenter; and debriefing by the group's facilitator.

In a consultancy protocol, for example, a teacher-presenter selects a piece of student work he or she has concerns about to share with the group. Led by a facilitator, the group has established norms for how they work and converse together. The presenter frames a question about the work to help participants focus their observations and discussions. For example, Ms. Wilkes, in the vignette, brought in a sampling of student persuasive essays and asked her colleagues how she could help her students develop more deliberate arguments. After the group examines the work with the framing question in mind, they ask questions to clarify and probe the presenter's concerns. This done, the group talks among themselves using descriptive, not critical, language about the work and suggests strategies to address the presenter's concerns. During this time, the presenter is an active listener, but not a participant. Next, the presenter responds to what he or she has heard, and a whole-group discussion follows. At the end, the facilitator summarizes the conversation, which might include suggestions on how to make the student work/teacher assignment better and how to place it within a context of the teaching and learning goals of the whole school.

Looking at Student and Teacher Work: Beginning the Process

When teachers first begin using protocols as a way of looking at their students' work, teacher assignments, and instructional practices, the process may feel formal or stiff. Because teachers are not used to sharing work publicly with peers, the process can feel intimidating. However, with time and practice the protocols create a safe, nurturing environment for teachers to make public their students' and their own work. As teachers gain experience, their comfort level rises, as do the benefits.

Many protocols have two rules that often cause discomfort among participants until they get used to them. One rule restricts when the presenting teacher has a turn to talk and when the group giving feedback can talk. At first, being told "you can't talk now" makes almost everyone feel awkward. But soon, participants see the benefits to careful, active listening.

The other rule governs the segment of the protocol when those giving feedback talk about the presenter; they use the third person, as if the presenter weren't in the room. Again, although this practice may seem unusual at first, the benefits to being able to listen without needing to respond or participate soon become apparent.

Ideally, everyone in the school community is involved in looking at student work. As the school community sets learning goals, they must look beyond standardized test scores to the daily work and exhibition projects that students produce.

What Work Should You Bring?

There are many kinds of student work to bring to a session for discussion. Make sure to bring the teacher assignment, directions, or prompt given to the students along with the criteria or rubric used to assess the work. Below are some examples of student work.

- Written work or artwork from several students in response to the same assignment
- Several pieces of work from one student in response to different assignments
- One piece of work from a student who you think completed the assignment successfully and another from a student who did not complete the same assignment successfully
- Work done by groups of students (at least two groups)
- Videotape, audiotape, and/or photographs of students working or presenting their work

Which Protocol Should You Use?

The purpose of looking at student work will dictate the details about the process: how much time it will take, who is involved, and how frequently the process is used. Academic teams who share the same groups of students usually look at student work on a weekly basis. However, throughout the school year it is also important for other teams, such as discipline-based teams, study groups, the school-site council, and the Leadership Team, to regularly use the protocols' work to inform their decisions.

The protocols for looking at student and teacher work have varying purposes. Some analyze what student work demonstrates about student learning, while others solve particular instructional dilemmas. As teachers work with the protocols, they may modify them to fit specific time requirements or to help teachers and administrators examine the work more closely. At first, using protocols may feel artificial and limiting; however, teachers soon find that protocols help them mine the riches that student work contains. Through the use of protocols, teachers clarify problems, identify evidence to support opinions, share perspectives, and reflect on their practice.

General Guidelines for All Protocols

Before a group uses protocols to look at student and teacher work, it is helpful to review the following guidelines with all participants.

Norms for Participants

- Be respectful of teacher-presenters. By making their work more public, teachers are taking a risk. As colleagues expose themselves and their work to peer review, remember to be thoughtful in how you word your responses.
- Contribute to the substance of the discussion. Thoughtful, probing questions and comments are beneficial. "Cool" questions enable participants to take the work to a deeper level.
- Be aware of "airtime." Protocols sometimes run on a tight schedule. Try to keep your comments succinct and relevant to the discussion.
- Be respectful of the facilitator's role. Do this especially in regard to keeping time and following protocol guidelines.

Guidelines for Facilitators

- Be assertive about keeping time. Each part of a protocol is crucial to the success of the exercise. Make sure you allow time for all parts of the protocol.
- Be protective of teacher-presenters. Many teachers may not be used to colleagues' critiquing their work. Try to determine just how "tough" your presenter wants the feedback to be. Inappropriate comments or questions should be recast or withdrawn.
- Be provocative of substantive discourse. While "warm" (see below) feedback is supportive, it often doesn't push a presenter's thinking. Encourage probing, "cool" questions and comments for a more beneficial protocol experience.

Feedback and Questions During Protocols

All participants in a protocol need to be considerate about how they speak, paying careful attention to the way they phrase their questions and comments for feedback.

"Warm" feedback and questions are positive comments and questions often used to begin the conversation. They are supportive and encouraging and put the presenter at ease. Examples:

What are the strengths of this work?

What's the good news here?

In what ways has (the teacher) encouraged students to . . . ?

I like the way he/she has . . . .

"Cool" feedback and questions often follow the "warm" questions and are more challenging, as participants voice doubts and ask questions about the work. Examples:

I wonder if you've considered . . . .

Have you thought about . . . ?

Where are the gaps?

I wonder what would happen if you tried . . . .

PEER OBSERVATION

Math teacher Melanie Turner watched over her tenth graders as they worked together on group projects. Although she always had a balance of academically strong and weak students in these cooperative learning groups and switched group roles for each new project, the groups always resorted to the same pattern, in which the strong, outgoing students took over. She wondered if she were doing something wrong, and if there were some way she could better facilitate this process.

At the end of the day, she decided to ask a colleague, Oscar Sanchez, to do a formal peer observation. He agreed. In a preobservation conference, Melanie told Oscar about her concern and asked him to focus his observations both on the group dynamics of her student groups and on her role as teacher.

Several days later Oscar came to Melanie's classroom, clipboard in hand, ready to observe and take notes. His peer observation revealed that Melanie unknowingly fed into the group dynamics she was unhappy with by always addressing her comments to the "strong" students in each group. Oscar also noticed that, although the students understood their roles as recorder, reporter, observer, and facilitator, they did not have the tools necessary to carry out these roles successfully.

In a debriefing conference, Oscar presented his findings to Melanie. Together they brainstormed solutions to the problem for Melanie to try out the next time she used cooperative learning groups.

Peer observation is one of the most powerful tools of a professional collaborative culture. In peer observation, teachers observe their colleagues in a structured, supportive way in order to improve student learning. When teachers teach in isolated classrooms, there is little opportunity to get feedback on how one is doing or to learn from each other. Without the stimulation that comes with such collegial discourse, many teachers stick with the same old lessons and instructional techniques they've always used. Lacking an ongoing infusion of new ideas and support from colleagues, many teachers become dispirited and frustrated when their students don't make progress.

Peer observation can help teachers become more effective as practitioners, thereby increasing job satisfaction and improving student achievement. Schools are broadening the definition of professional development to include more flexible approaches to building staff knowledge and skills, and many are using peer observation as part of a comprehensive professional development plan.

What Happens During Peer Observation?

Peer observation is a three-part collaborative process in which teachers observe and are observed by each other in order to improve their practice.

Part 1: Before the Observation

Part 1 takes place before the actual observation, when the observer and the teacher to be observed meet. During this meeting, the observed teacher tells his or her colleague(s) what the observer(s) should focus on in the classroom. The focus of the observation might be a particular student, student interactions within a group, the lesson, teaching techniques, or teacher/student interactions. The observed teacher tells the observer(s) what is going to happen in class on the day of the observation and what the observer(s) should pay attention to. Together, they clarify the purpose of the observation.

Part 2: During the Observation

At the time of the observation, the observed teacher introduces the observer to the students and explains why he or she is there. During the observation, the observer records what he or she sees, keeping in mind the agreed-upon focus of the observation. Observations are descriptive phrases that answer questions such as, *What is the teacher doing or saying? What are the students doing or saying?* Examples of reflections and questions are: *Students seem confused—why? Are there other ways to present material?* In addition, the observer should note time intervals.

Part 3: After the Observation

Just as important as parts 1 and 2 is the thirty- to forty-five-minute debriefing session that follows soon after the observation. In this part, the observing teacher(s) and the observed teacher together reconstruct what happened during the observation. Focusing on the goals of the observation, they each talk about what they felt went well during the class and what they might change. The observed teacher asks for specific descriptions and constructive feedback, and the observer describes rather than evaluates what he or she saw.

Benefits of Peer Observation

As teachers observe their colleagues and discuss what they've seen in a structured, supportive way, they derive many benefits:

- Learning about students—how they respond to different subject areas, instructional methods, and grade levels; perform in different learning environments; display different learning styles; interact in pairs and within groups; interact with the teacher; and ask and answer questions.
- Becoming aware of the physical environment and its match with instruction.
- Examining instructional materials in relation to teaching and learning.
- Receiving a critical, focused analysis of different aspects of teaching.
- Being exposed to new ideas and ways of teaching to try in the classroom.
- Modeling collaborative practices for students.

Developing Skills for Peer Observation

Just as teachers need to take care in how they give feedback to colleagues while working and when using protocols for looking at student and teacher work, they also need to develop similar skills for peer observation. Before engaging in the peer observation protocols, teachers should be familiar with their different purposes and processes. They should also be aware of and have practice in using the essential skills of active listening and observing, using descriptive rather than evaluative language and moving from positive to challenging comments.

DATA-BASED INQUIRY AND ACTION RESEARCH

At an academic team meeting in late November, four teachers from Wilson High School's tenth-grade team were using a protocol to look at samples of student essays, analyzing the changes between first and final drafts. They framed a question to focus their discussion: What evidence do we see that shows improvement between the first and final drafts of these essays? After careful analysis and discussion, they decided that there wasn't much evidence at all that showed improvement between drafts.

"It looks like they just moved a couple of sentences around, corrected their spelling errors, and copied the essay over," said one teacher. "They don't get what revision is all about."

"Maybe it's because we're not being effective in showing them," offered another teacher.

Together, the team decided to do a data-based inquiry research project to see how they were currently teaching writing, so they could find ways to improve it. They stated the problem this way: Final drafts of student essays do not show evidence of a careful revision process. Then they formed the research question: How can we help students make improvements between first and final drafts of essays? To study the problem, they made a plan to collect data that included peer observations, observations of students at work in peer-editing groups ("shadow" studies), and more writing samples. One month later, after completing the data collection phase of action research, they sat down to analyze what they'd collected. Among their findings were the following: (1) students hadn't received enough training in how to give feedback in their peer-editing groups; (2) a formal process didn't exist for teachers to meet in one-on-one conferences with their students; and (3) many students were not engaged with the essay topics they were assigned.

The teachers then proposed solutions to the problems. They agreed to set aside a block of time to practice the peer-editing process with students, they outlined a process by which they would work with students individually, and they made a commitment to allowing students more choice in what they wanted to write about.

Achieving equity is a fundamental goal of all small schools—to ensure high levels of achievement for all students, particularly those from student groups that have historically had less access to a challenging curriculum and have experienced lower achievement than more privileged students. Equity can best be addressed using data-based inquiry.

Data-Based Inquiry

Small schools engage in data-based inquiry and decision making to learn about how the school is run, to find ways to improve the school, and to promote equity among students. Data-based inquiry and decision making is a deliberate process in which teachers, administrators, students, parents, and other community members collect, examine, and analyze a range of data relating to problems and challenges, and develop action plans to address them. This process is particularly valuable in small schools, where expectations for learning are not confined to students but extend to all members of the school community. People are always asking questions about how the school is doing so they can make things better. For example, are students really building math and literacy skills? Is the time scheduled for team meetings adequate and productive? What do student work and statewide test scores reveal about equity for all the different groups within our school?

Data-based inquiry focuses on the challenges that most impact learning, teaching, and assessment. It allows teachers to work together to pose questions about their practice, collect data relative to their questions, analyze the data, and then make changes in their practice based on that analysis. While teachers may study what others are doing or have done to inform their practice, they may also want to take a look at what they are doing in their own classrooms in order to improve it. In data-based inquiry, teachers set the agenda: they identify something they want to study to improve teaching and learning. Because they choose issues of personal interest rather than having goals imposed upon them, they are more committed to the goals they set for themselves.

Data-based inquiry involves a continuous cycle of inquiry that aims at changing instructional practice. After teachers form questions about what they want to study, collect and analyze data, and make improvements in their practice as a result of their research, they repeat the cycle by raising new or refined questions. As teachers try out new ideas and instructional strategies, this "cycle of inquiry" provides regular opportunities for reflection. When data-based inquiry is conducted in collaborative groups, teachers have opportunities to receive ongoing feedback from colleagues as they attempt new instructional strategies. They also have the opportunity to investigate and share findings on how changes in practice affect student learning.

Often, data-based inquiry starts at the school level, with gaining a picture of what is going well and what the challenges are within a school. This initial process of "taking a picture" of the school is then used to pursue identified challenges, understand their underlying causes, and develop solutions and action plans that can address them. Alternatively, teacher teams that have already identified an instructional dilemma they would like to pursue engage in data-based inquiry by entering the process at the stage of problem formation described below.

Steps of the Data-Based Inquiry Process

The cycle of data-based inquiry includes the following elements:

Set the vision: Data-based inquiry is always based on the school's articulated vision of what effective instruction and student learning should look like (see Tool 7.4, "Developing a Vision Statement").

Collect and analyze data: Gather multiple sources of data that will give a comprehensive picture of the school and the students that are served. Possible sources of data include achievement data; suspension, attendance, grade retention, dropout, graduation, and college-going rates; enrollment in high-level and remedial classes as well as special education; surveys, observations, and interviews; curriculum materials; student and teacher work; and pertinent education research. Always try to disaggregate data by subgroup, including by race, income, gender, special education status, and English language learners.

Identify successes and challenges: Examine all of the data and use them to identify: (1) the school's successes, or the areas in which the school is doing well, and (2) the challenges, or areas in which the school needs to improve. Once a synthesized list has been developed, a school's faculty and administration can decide on how to highlight and celebrate their successes and identify the priority challenges that are worthy of further data-based inquiry. These challenges should be those that, if solved, would most improve student learning and achievement.

Once a priority challenge has been determined, faculty study groups take on individual challenges to pursue. These study groups are empowered to engage in a process of further inquiry that will lead them to identify the underlying causes of their assigned challenge area and develop solutions and an action plan to present to the full faculty for discussion and approval prior to implementation.

Problem formation: Using the challenge area that the group is pursuing, develop a research question. Research questions should be specific enough that they are solvable and, if solved, will significantly improve student learning.

Criteria for action research questions include:

- Questions should be focused on an instructional dilemma.
- Questions should not have "yes/no" answers.
- Questions should help explore the nature of the problem.
- Questions' phrasing should avoid evaluative words.
- Assumptions and terms embedded in the questions should be clarified.
- Questions should strike a balance between being narrow and open-ended.
- Avoid "why" questions.
- Those involved should not already know the answer to the question.
- Those involved must be passionate about the question.

Develop hypotheses: Brainstorm all of the potential reasons for why the problem could exist.

Data collection: Collect data on your research that will help prove or disprove your list of hypotheses. Also, read available research about your instructional dilemma.

Determine the cause of the problem: Analyze data and determine causes of the question or problem. This is a key step in the cycle of data-based inquiry. If you do not identify the real cause of the problem, you will not necessarily select the best solution.

Determine solutions: Based on your analysis of the data and the causes of the problem that you identified, determine possible changes that will effectively address the question or problem.

Action plan: Develop and implement an action plan based on the solution to the question or problem. At some point, present findings and propose a plan to the full faculty for their discussion and approval.

Assessment: Assess the impact of the solution on improving student learning, and make refinements.

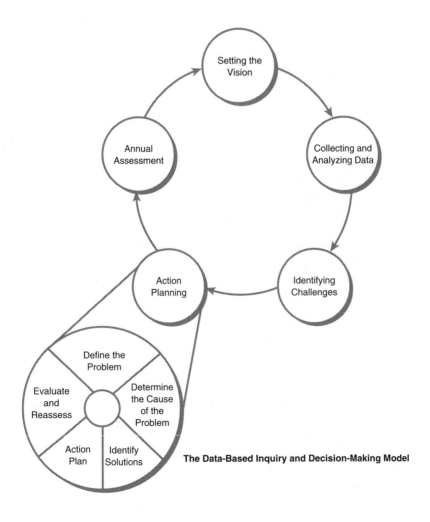

The Data-Based Inquiry and Decision-Making Model

TOOLS FOR THE PRACTICE OF A COLLABORATIVE CULTURE

The following tools will help teams build a professional collaborative culture. The tools and techniques, or protocols, in this section are culled from a variety of sources and, according to Joseph P. McDonald (2001), "while designed and promoted by particular organizations, belong to the community of teachers at large" (p. 215).

Our work is largely informed by the initial efforts of the Coalition of Essential Schools, and the subsequent work of the National School Reform Faculty (NSRF) and the Looking at Student Work Collaborative. It is in the spirit of the ongoing commitments and efforts of these organizations that we present these tools and techniques that will contribute to and benefit all schools as they build professional collaborative cultures. We include a small set of protocols in this guide. Many more are available at the NSRF Web site (http://www.nsrfharmony.org).

Table 8.1   Protocols

Name of Protocol	When to Use It	What Work to Bring
Consultancy Protocol	To get feedback on a question or concerns posed by a teacher regarding certain aspects of student or teacher work.	Written reflection by presenter. A question to focus the feedback. Student work that illustrates the question or concern.
Tuning Protocol	To develop more effective curriculum plans, assignments, or assessments. To develop common standards for students' work. To reflect on and gather ideas for revision of classroom practice.	Student work reflecting a final exhibition or long-term project; may include a videotape of a student presentation and a written piece. The assignment or lesson material before it is given to students.
Charrette	To get feedback on a process or piece of work when the teacher, student, or group is experiencing difficulty, or when additional minds could help it move forward.	Any "work in progress."
Critical Incident Protocol	For a teacher to reflect with colleagues on a particularly significant or compelling incident from his or her work, in order to gain new insights into teacher practice and student work.	A written piece by the presenter that tells about the incident in as much detail as possible.
Reviewing a Slice of Writing	To obtain a focused analysis of certain characteristics of student writing.	A selection of student writing, previously scored "low," "medium," and "high," from several teachers.

Tool 8.1: Consultancy Protocol

Purpose: To get feedback on a set of questions or concerns posed by a teacher about certain aspects of student or teacher work.

Directions: A presenter and a facilitator work with a group of participants to examine student or teacher work.

Step 1. The presenter gives a quick overview of the work, highlighting the major issues or problems with which he or she is struggling, and frames a question for the consultancy group to consider. The framing of this question, as well as the quality of the presenter's reflections on the work and/or issue being discussed, are key features of this protocol. (10 minutes)

Step 2. The consultancy group asks clarifying questions (questions that have brief, factual answers) of the presenter. (5 minutes)

Step 3. The group then asks probing questions of the presenter. These questions should be worded to help the presenter clarify and expand his or her thinking about the issue or questions that he or she has raised for the consultancy group. The goal here is for the presenter to learn more about the question he or she framed or to do some analysis of the issue presented. The presenter responds to the group's questions, but there is no discussion by the larger group of the presenter's responses. (10–15 minutes)

Step 4. The group then discusses the work and issues presented. What did we hear? What didn't we hear that we need to know about? What do we think about the question or issue presented? Some groups like to begin the conversation with "warm" feedback, answering questions such as "What are the strengths in this situation or in this student's work?" "What's the good news here?" The group then moves on to "cooler" feedback, answering questions such as "Where are the gaps?" "What isn't the presenter considering?" "What might be areas for further improvement or investigation?" Sometimes the group will raise questions for the presenter to consider: "I wonder what would happen if . . . ?" "I wonder why . . . ?" The presenter is not allowed to speak during this discussion, but instead listens and takes notes. (15 minutes)

Step 5. The presenter then responds to what he or she has heard. A whole-group discussion might then take place, depending on the time allotted. (10–15 minutes)

Step 6. The facilitator leads a brief discussion about the group's observations of the process. (5–10 minutes)

Some Tips for Consultancies

Step 1: The success of the consultancy often depends on the quality of the presenter's reflection in step 1, as well as on the quality and authenticity of the question framed for the

(Continued)

(Continued)

consultancy group. However, it is not uncommon for a presenter to say at the end of a consultancy, "Now I know what my real question is." That is fine, too. It is sometimes helpful for the presenter to prepare ahead of time a brief (one- or two-page) written description of the issues for the consultancy group to read as part of step 1.

Steps 2 and 3: Clarifying questions are for the person asking them. They ask the presenter "Who, what, where, when, and how." These are not "why" questions. They can be answered quickly and succinctly, often with a phrase or two.

Probing questions are for the person answering them. They ask the presenter "why" (among other things) and are open-ended. They take longer to answer and often require deep thought on the part of the presenter.

Step 4: When the group talks, it is helpful for the presenter to pull her/his chair back slightly away from the group. This protocol requires the consultancy group to talk about the presenter in the third person, almost as if he or she were not there. As awkward as this may feel at first, it often opens up a rich conversation. Remember that it is the group's job to offer an analysis of the issue or question presented. It is not necessary to solve the problem or to offer a definitive answer.

It is important for the presenter to listen in a non-defensive manner. The presenter should listen for new ideas, perspectives, and approaches and listen to the group's analysis of his or her question/issues. The presenter should listen for assumptions—both his or hers and the group's—implicit in the conversation. The presenter should also be alert for judgment by the group; this is not supposed to be about the presenter, but about a question he or she has raised. The presenter should remember that he or she asked the group to help with this question or issue.

Step 5: The point of this time period is not for the presenter to give a "blow-by-blow" response to the group's conversation, nor is it to defend or further explain. Rather, this is a time for the presenter to talk about what were, for him or her, the most significant comments, ideas, and questions heard. The presenter can also share any new thoughts or questions he or she has had while listening to the consultancy group.

Step 6: Debriefing the process is key. Do not shortchange this step.

SOURCE: Used with permission of the National School Reform Faculty (NSRF), Harmony Education Center, Bloomington, IN (http://www.nsrfharmony.org).

Tool 8.2: Tuning Protocol

Purpose: To develop more effective exhibitions and assessments.

Directions: Often the presenting teacher begins with a focusing question or area about which she or he would especially welcome feedback—for example, "Are you seeing evidence of persuasive writing in the student's work?" or "Does this lesson accommodate different learning styles?" The overarching purpose of a tuning protocol is to give teachers critical feedback on a single aspect of their practice, either through their own work or the work of their students.

Participation in a structured process of professional collaboration like this can be intimidating and anxiety producing, especially for the teacher presenting work. Having a shared set of guidelines or norms helps everybody participate in a manner that is respectful as well as conducive to helpful feedback.

Guidelines

- Be respectful of teacher-presenters. By making their work more public, teachers are exposing themselves to kinds of critiques they may not be used to. Inappropriate comments or questions should be reworded or withdrawn.
- Contribute to substantive discussion. Many teachers may be used to blanket praise. Without thoughtful, probing, "cool" questions and comments, teachers will not benefit from the tuning protocol.
- Be respectful of the facilitator's role, particularly in regard to following the guidelines and keeping time. A tuning protocol that doesn't allow for all parts (presentation, feedback, response, debrief) will do a disservice to the teacher-presenters and to the participants.

Schedule for Tuning Protocol

1. **Introduction**—Protocol goals, guidelines, and schedule. (5–10 minutes)

2. **Teacher presentation**—Context for work, focusing question; group is silent. (10–15 minutes)

3. **Clarifying questions**—This is not the time for warm/cool feedback. (5 minutes maximum)

4. **Examination of work sample(s)** (5–15 minutes)

5. **Pause for reflections**—Participants reflect on potential contribution. (2–3 minutes)

6. **Warm and cool feedback**—Group shares feedback; presenter is silent. (15 minutes)

7. **Reflection**—Presenter speaks to issue(s) deemed appropriate. (10–15 minutes)

8. **Debrief**—Open discussion on the experiences of the group. (10 minutes)

SOURCE: The Tuning Protocol was originally developed as a means for the five high schools in the Coalition of Essential School's Exhibitions Project to receive feedback and fine-tune their developing student assessment systems, including exhibitions, portfolios, and design projects. It has since been adapted as a tool for looking collaboratively at both teachers' and students' work, and used extensively in the work of the National School Reform Faculty. Used with permission of the National School Reform Faculty (NSRF), Harmony Education Center, Bloomington, IN (http://www.nsrfharmony.org).

Tool 8.3: Charrette

Purpose: To get feedback on a work in progress when a teacher, student, or group is "stuck."

Background: Charrette is a term and process borrowed from the architectural community. The purpose of a charrette is to improve a piece of work. A team uses this protocol when the members have reached a point in looking at teacher and student work where they cannot easily move forward on their own.

Charrettes are not normally held during the final exhibition of work or at the completion of a project; they are not culminating assessments or final evaluations. Instead, they are held in a low-stakes/no-stakes environment, where the requesting team has much to gain from the process and virtually nothing to lose. In short, charrettes are used to scrutinize and improve work before it is ever placed in a high-stakes environment.

Directions

1. A group or an individual from the group requests a charrette when one or more of the following conditions exist:
   a. the group is experiencing difficulty with the work
   b. a stopping point has been reached
   c. additional minds (thinkers new to the work) could help move it forward

2. A second group, ranging in size from three to six people, is formed to look at the work. A moderator/facilitator is designated from the newly formed group. It is the moderator's job to observe the charrette, record information that is being created, ask questions along the way, and occasionally summarize the discussion.

3. The requesting team presents its "work in progress" while the other group listens. (There are no strict time limits, but this usually takes five to ten minutes.)

4. The requesting team states what it needs or wants from the charrette, thereby accepting the responsibility of focusing the discussion. This focus usually takes the form of a specific request, but it can be as generic as, "How can we make this better?" or "What is our next step?"

5. The invited group then discusses while the requesting team listens and takes notes. There are no hard and fast rules here. Occasionally (but not usually) the requesting team joins in the discussion process. The emphasis is on improving the work, which now belongs to the entire group, both the requesting and the invited team. The atmosphere is one of "we're in this together," with the single purpose of "making a good thing even better."

6. When the members of the requesting group know they have gotten what they need from the invited group, they stop the process, briefly summarize what was gained, thank the participants and moderator, and return to the drawing board.

SOURCE: Adapted from Kathy Juarez, Piner High School, Santa Rosa, CA. Used with permission of the National School Reform Faculty (NSRF), Harmony Education Center, Bloomington, IN (http://www.nsrfharmony.org).

Tool 8.4: Critical Incident Protocol

Purpose: To provide an opportunity for a teacher to reflect with colleagues on an incident from his or her work that was particularly rewarding, puzzling, or devastating in order to gain new insights into teacher practice and student learning.

Directions: Assign a facilitator for each round. The facilitator's role is to keep the conversation moving through each phase and to facilitate the final conversation. The facilitator should also keep time.

The "learner," or presenter, presents a critical incident from and within the context of his or her work as a text for learning. The learner also frames a professional outcome toward which he or she is working. The group listens carefully to understand the incident and the context, and then asks clarifying questions. As the learner listens, the "friends" then discuss and raise questions as advocates for the learner's success. The learner responds, and the group talks together about the content and/or process of the conversation.

1. Learner presents critical incident. (10 minutes)

2. Friends ask clarifying questions. (5 minutes)

3. Friends raise questions, note the significance of the incident in the context of the learner's work, and discuss as advocates. Learner listens. (15 minutes)

4. Learner responds. Then the group engages in general conversation about the content and/or process. (15 minutes)

5. Debrief the process. (5 minutes)

SOURCE: This formal process for critical friendship uses a variation of the model described in A. Costa and B. Kallick (1993), Through the lens of a critical friend, *Educational Leadership, 51*(2), pp. 49–81. Reprinted with permission of the National School Reform Faculty (NSRF), Harmony Education Center, Bloomington, IN (http://www.nsrfharmony.org).

Tool 8.5: Reviewing a Slice of Writing

Purpose: To conduct a focused analysis of certain aspects of previously scored student writing samples.

Directions

Gather the Writing Slice

Gather samples of student writing from several teachers for analysis. Each sample should be the result of using the same writing prompt across a grade span, a grade level, or the curriculum. Samples should be scored by students' individual teachers before the descriptive review. Include one "high," one "medium," and one "low" sample from each teacher. One sample should be from an English Language Learner (ELL) student. If there are too many samples, eliminate the "medium" sample, but keep the ELL sample. Cover or remove all student names and scores.

Set-Up

Everyone gets the same paginated packet of student work.

Everyone speaks in each round. Rounds can go clockwise or counterclockwise.

Everyone speaks in turn and describes ONE thing, and only ONE thing he or she sees in the writing.

Facilitation is "intrusive"—keeping each round of descriptions at a particular level, while keeping things moving quickly. There is no discussion at this time.

Facilitation includes a short recap of one or more rounds, if appropriate.

The facilitator may ask participants to pause and reflect between some rounds (e.g., a brief period of writing).

Process

Times are adjustable depending on the time available.

Explain the process. Introduce and briefly discuss the framing question.
(e.g., What are the characteristics of proficient writing?) (5 minutes).

Participants examine the writing samples, looking for evidence of proficient writing.

They take notes, listing the page number and specific examples for reference during the discussions.
(15+ minutes)

The facilitator takes close notes of participant responses during the rounds. (30+ minutes)

The facilitator leads a final debrief of the process; this includes answering the question, "What have we learned of value from looking at this work and why?"
Findings are recorded for comparison with future "slices."

SOURCE: Used with permission of the National School Reform Faculty (NSRF), Harmony Education Center, Bloomington, IN (http://www.nsrfharmony.org).

Tool 8.6: Video Camera

Purpose: To develop observational reliability between the observer and the observed.

Directions: An underlying assumption is that no two people observing the same event will see the same thing, as the perceptions and prior experiences of each act as a filter. This protocol provides a way for the observed and the observer to discover what the other "sees" during the observation and to help each learn to see as much as possible.

1. **Preobservation conference:** The person to be observed outlines what will occur during the observation. At this point, a facilitator should be selected to run the postobservation discussion.

2. **Observation:** Observers watch the lesson, class, performance, etc. To the greatest extent possible, each observer acts like a video camera, scripting and making note of as many events as possible. Care should be taken not to attempt to interpret or question during the observation.

3. **Affirmation:** Observers talk about what they appreciated and valued with questions and comments such as

   - What meaning did this have for me?

   - What is honest and true for me as a responder?

   - When you did such and such, it was evocative, challenging, unique, etc.

4. **Questions and conversation:** The presenter, or person who has been observed, asks specific questions. Usually the presenter has the same questions as the observers do; when the presenter starts the dialogue, the opportunity for honesty increases. Observers answer questions and formulate questions in return, trying to be neutral (not "Why didn't you do it differently?" but "What did you have in mind when you chose to present the lesson in this way?"). This approach increases the likelihood of hearing what others are saying and actually learning from it.

5. **Response and discussion:** Observers respond to the presenter's questions, leading to discussion of the substance of the lesson or performance. Observers offer opinions freely but should ask the presenter for permission to be critical. Most reactions to the work that are formulated as mature criticism are actually merely opinions. These can be used to weave one's own solution, but they may be hard for the person being observed to hear or to use. Personal stories can be included here—examples from observers' classrooms that connect with the presenter's questions.

6. **Next steps:** What are the next steps for the presenter to improve the lesson, performance, etc.? The presenter may now state a particular dilemma. Suggestion: this can be a conversation between the presenter and the facilitator, with the others watching.

7. **Debrief:** During the first part of the debriefing, one observer reconstructs the observation from her notes. The observed should listen carefully, taking note of any details that escaped her notice and jotting down anything remembered that is not mentioned by the observer. The observed speaks during the second phase of the debriefing, naming those details of which she was not aware and adding her own.

SOURCE: Used with permission of the National School Reform Faculty (NSRF), Harmony Education Center, Bloomington, IN (http://www.nsrfharmony.org).

NOTE: It is important that both parties refrain from interpretation. To say that the student was bored is very different from saying that the student drew circles and designs in the margins of papers, yawned, and looked out the window. Value statements ("That was a great lesson") should also be avoided.

Tool 8.7: Focus Point

Purpose: To help deepen the observed teacher's understanding of his or her practice.

Directions: The observer's role is to note those events that relate to a particular aspect of the observer's practice and then to serve as an active listener as the observed attempts to make sense of those events.

1. **Preobservation conference:** In addition to outlining what will be occurring during the observation, the person to be observed asks the observer to focus on a particular aspect of his practice. Example: "Would you look at how I respond to student questions?"

2. **Observation:** The observer focuses on the aspect of practice raised during the preobservation conference. Field notes include both descriptions of "focus" events and related questions that the observer may want to raise during the debriefing. (The observer may also want to note events and questions outside the focus of the observation, but these may or may not be discussed during the debriefing.)

3. **Debriefing:** The observer begins by restating the focus and asking the observed teacher to share his or her thoughts. Example: "What did you notice about how you responded to student questions?" As the observed talks, the observer may (1) supply specific events that either corroborate or contrast with the observed teacher's statements, (2) summarize what the observed is saying, (3) ask clarifying questions, or (4) raise focus-related questions that were noted during the observation.

SOURCE: Used with permission of the National School Reform Faculty (NSRF), Harmony Education Center, Bloomington, IN (http://www.nsrfharmony.org).

NOTE: Events and questions not directly related to the focus of the observation should be raised only after asking for permission from the observed teacher, and some practitioners think even asking for permission is inappropriate. The observer should refrain from stating his or her ideas and perspective on the issues unless specifically invited to do so.

Tool 8.8: Interesting Moments

Purpose: To have a shared experience where the observer and presenter work together during both the observation and the debriefing.

Directions: The underlying assumption for this protocol is that the observer and the observed will work together to create some new knowledge—they are in it together. The observation is a shared experience, and so is the debriefing. One outsider, after listening to such a debriefing, stated that it was a seamless conversation: "The two of you were discovering something about the events you had seen."

1. **Preobservation conference:** Because this form of observation is more open-ended, it is not strictly necessary to have a preobservation conference, although it may help to orient the observer as to what will be happening.

2. **Observation:** The observer maintains an open field of vision, noting anything that strikes him or her as particularly interesting—anything that may lead to "deep" questions.

3. **Debriefing:** Either participant begins by raising a point of interest, stating as clearly and as fully as possible what occurred. A conversation develops around the incident, with both observer and observed attempting to sort out "What was going on there?" As the ideas build, both are responsible for keeping the conversation on track while maintaining the flexibility necessary to create new understandings.

SOURCE: Used with permission of the National School Reform Faculty (NSRF), Harmony Education Center, Bloomington, IN (http://www.nsrfharmony.org).

NOTE: Prerequisite for this protocol is a high level of trust between the two participants—trust that the debriefing is not about evaluation; trust that each will be thoughtful and will listen and respond to the other; trust that whatever knowledge is created will be shared knowledge.

Tool 8.9: Teaming

Purpose: To share planning and implementation of lesson(s) to be taught.

Directions: In the "Interesting Moments" protocol, the debriefing process is more of a shared activity; both participants searched for some understanding, trying to create meaning. In this version, the participants also share the planning and implementation of the lesson(s) to be taught. Utilizing either a form of parallel teaching or a more seamless coteaching, the participants are both "on" with the students. Both are observers and observed.

1. **Preobservation conference:** This takes the form of a planning session. Issues of outcomes, goals, objectives, and assessment are discussed, and the activity is planned. If the two participants will be coteaching and one or both are unfamiliar with the art of teaching with a partner, special attention should be paid to the issue of who will do what and how they will interact when working with the students.

2. **Observation:** It is important that some form of observational notes be taken. In a coteaching situation, some people carry a clipboard or notebook as they move around the classroom, taking time to note anything of interest. Others feel this distracts them (or their students) and prefer to write as soon as possible after the event. A third method would be to videotape the session and use the playback during the debriefing. (Warning: the use of video needs to be considered carefully. Among other consequences, it creates the need for a longer debriefing period.)

3. **Debriefing:** As with the "Interesting Moments" protocol, either participant begins by raising a point of interest, stating as dearly and as fully as possible what occurred. A conversation develops around the incident, with both observer and observed attempting to sort out "What was going on there?"

SOURCE: Used with permission of the National School Reform Faculty (NSRF), Harmony Education Center, Bloomington, IN (http://www.nsrfharmony.org).

NOTE: Despite research that extols the benefits of team teaching (as opposed to team planning), this pedagogy is a break with the cultural norm of isolation that exists in most schools. Even though many who participate in long-term team teaching find it exhilarating and the best form of staff development, it is not often done.

Tool 8.10: Observer as Learner

Purpose: To use observation as a means to learn how to improve one's own practice.

Directions: The primary "learner" in this protocol is the observer. The observer's only purpose is to learn how to improve her practice. Since the observer has little responsibility to the observed teacher, the duration of the observation, and even the level of attention to what's going on, is determined by the observer, as long as this is fine with the person being observed. The time involved may also be reduced if neither party desires a preobservation conference.

1. **Preobservation conference:** It is not necessary to have a preobservation conference unless either party would like to have one. A preobservation conference would help to orient the observer as to what will be happening.

2. **Observation:** The observer focuses on whatever she wishes.

3. **Debriefing:** The observer often asks the observed questions that might help her better understand the choices made by the observed.

SOURCE: Used with permission of the National School Reform Faculty (NSRF), Harmony Education Center, Bloomington, IN (http://www.nsrfharmony.org).

NOTE: Given the potential feeling of vulnerability on the part of the observed teacher in any situation, and especially in a situation such as this, where the observed teacher may have little idea of what the observer is focusing on, it's important that during the debriefing the observer try to ask questions in a way that does not put the observed teacher on the defensive.

Tool 8.11: Peer Observation Record

Purpose: To provide a way to record observations, reflections, questions, and other data during peer observation.

Directions: Use this form as a record during a peer observation.

Preobservation Meeting

Research question:

Observed teacher's goals for the visit:

The Visit

Observations:

Reflections/Questions:

Debriefing the Visit

Key ideas and reflections:

Implications for future practice:

Tool 8.12: Continuum on Using Data for Equity and Excellence

Purpose: To help participants assess how their school currently uses data for equity and excellence, and to suggest that a more systemic and deliberate process of using data can better address equity and excellence in their schools.

Directions

Continuum Activity: Using chairs, tape, or chart paper spaced along a wall, mark the room off as a continuum with the labels *strongly agree, agree, disagree, strongly disagree.* Have participants stand along the continuum at the point that best matches individual responses to the statements below. Each time, ask those representing the opposite ends of the spectrum and the middle to state why they stood where they did.

Statements

- Our school has concrete goals regarding high achievement and equity for each student. The school uses data to track the performance of different groups of students (particularly historically low-achieving or underrepresented student populations).
- Our school regularly uses multiple sources of data (standardized tests, student work, attendance, suspensions, enrollment in high-level courses, surveys, classroom observations) to set and revise schoolwide goals with respect to equity and excellence.
- Faculty, administrators, parents, and students are involved in looking at data, identifying challenges, and setting schoolwide goals. The school leadership uses a collaborative process to ensure that all voices are engaged and heard.
- Our school has a well-developed and intentional system for collaborative decision making based on data. Committees have processes for gathering feedback and moving toward action plans based on an analysis of data, leading the school toward decisions that effect achievement and equity for all students.

Debriefing: After continuum activity, use the following three questions to debrief.

- What did you notice about where people are standing?
- What can you synthesize from this activity about how schools use data for equity and excellence?
- How can your school use data in a more systemic way?

SOURCE: The continuum activity was developed by staff at CCE. The statements were adapted from a 1999 survey on data-based inquiry and decision making developed by the High Performance Learning Communities Consortium (HPLC), which includes RPP International, California Tomorrow, and the Bay Area Coalition of Essential Schools (BAYCES).

Tool 8.13: Analyzing Data Chart

Purpose: To list strengths and challenges that you find within data and to group them according to the Small Schools Principles.

Directions: Use this chart to record data.

What Do the Data Say?		
Category Type	*Strengths*	*Challenges*
Equity and access: A school's goals apply to all students		
Habits of mind: Teaching students to use their minds well		
Personalization: The school is small and organized so that teachers and students know each other well		
Less is more: Each students is expected to master a limited number of essential skills and areas of knowledge		
Student-as-worker, teacher-as-coach: Teachers guide students in taking responsibility for their learning		

(Continued)

(Continued)

What Do the Data Say?		
Category Type	Strengths	Challenges
Assessment by exhibition: Students should demonstrate their mastery of competencies in various ways		
High expectations, trust, respect, and caring for all		
Professional collaborative communities: The principal and teachers serve multiple obligations and work together to create a professional collaborative learning community		
Flexibility, autonomy, and shared governance: The school has maximum flexibility and autonomy, enabling decisions to be made as close to the learner as possible		

Tool 8.14: Determining Possible Causes of the Problem

Purpose: To guide brainstorming, refining, testing, and selecting hypotheses as a way to identify two or three most likely causes of an identified problem.

Directions: Use this tool after a group has formed a question or problem in the "determine solutions" phase of action research.

Research question:

Brainstorm causes. Consider all possible reasons that the problem exists. Develop a list of hypotheses. The group should not expect to arrive at an immediate or single explanation for or cause of the problem.

Refine and test hypotheses. Review the list of hypotheses to eliminate those that are least likely to be the causes of the problem. Test those that are most plausible to confirm whether they are probable causes.

Hypothesis (Why does the problem exist?)	How will we test it?	After we test it, is the hypothesis feasible?
1.		
2.		
3.		
4.		
5.		
6.		

(Continued)

(Continued)

List causes. From the tested hypotheses, list one, two, or three most likely causes of the problem to be used in developing solutions.

Causes

1.

2.

3.

Tool 8.15: Action Planning Form

Purpose: To record a research question, proposed solutions, strategies/tasks/actions, person(s) responsible, timeline, and budget resources.

Directions: Use this form for action planning.

Group name:

Action research question or problem:

Proposed solutions: As you consider solutions, ask
- *Will the implementation of this solution address the problem?*
- *What are the potential obstacles?*
- *Is the solution practical?*
- *Are there enough resources?*

Strategies/ Tasks/Actions	Person(s) Responsible	Timeline	Budget/Resources

Conclusion

It seems fitting to end this guide with a focus on collaboration. With effective collaboration across schools and communities, the small schools strategy has enormous potential to transform the educational landscape. It is certainly true that for too long individual teachers, principals, superintendents, union officials, parents, and community leaders have worked in isolation from one another—and often at cross-purposes.

As we complete this guide, The Los Angeles Unified School District, in partnership with the union Unified Teachers Los Angeles, have launched a plan to establish up to ten small college-preparatory pilot high schools modeled after the Boston Pilot Schools. We are hopeful that many more cities will follow their example. We know what a challenging road lies ahead but also what exciting possibilities and student successes are within reach.

We hope *Creating Small Schools: A Handbook for Raising Equity and Achievement* will be a useful companion to all of those in districts, unions, and communities who are trying to offer students a better future by creating effective small schools.

References

Ballen, J., & Moles, O. (1994). *Strong families, strong schools: Building community partnerships for learning.* Washington, DC: U.S. Department of Education.

Bamber, C., Berla, N., & Henderson, A. T. (1996). Learning from others: Good programs and successful campaigns. Washington, DC: Center for Law and Education.

Bilby, S. (2002). Community school reform: Parents making a difference in education. *Mott Mosaic, 1*(2), 2–7.

Boston Public Schools/Boston Teachers Union High School Restructuring Task Force. (1998). Report. Boston: Author.

Canady, R., & Rettig, M. (1995). The power of innovative scheduling. *Educational Leadership, 53*(3), 4–10.

Center for Collaborative Education. (2006). *The essential guide to pilot schools: Overview.* Boston: Author.

Center for Collaborative Education. (2006). *Progress and promise: A report on the Boston Pilot Schools.* Boston: Author.

Center for Collaborative Education. (2005). *Understanding learning: Assessment in the Turning Points school.* Boston: Author.

Center for Collaborative Education. (2003). *At the Turning Point: The young adolescent learner.* Boston: Author.

Center for Collaborative Education. (2003). *Cherry Lane High case study: Restructuring a large, comprehensive high school to small schools.* Boston: Author.

Center for Collaborative Education. (2003). *Creating partnerships, bridging worlds: Family and community engagement.* Boston: Author.

Center for Collaborative Education. (2001). *Guide to collaborative culture and shared leadership.* Boston: Author.

Center for Collaborative Education. (2001). *Guide to data-based inquiry and decision making.* Boston: Author.

Center for Collaborative Education. (2001). *Looking collaboratively at student and teacher work.* Boston: Author.

Center for Collaborative Education. (2001). *School structures that support learning and collaboration.* Boston: Author.

Center for Collaborative Education. (2001). *Teaching literacy in the Turning Points school.* Boston: Author.

Center for Collaborative Education. (2001). *Turning Points guide to curriculum development.* Boston: Author.

Christenson, S. L., & Sheridan, S. M. (2001). *Schools and families: Creating essential connections for learning.* New York: Guilford.

Costa, A., & Kallick, B. (1993). Through the lens of a critical friend. *Educational Leadership, 51*(2), 49–81.

Cotton, K. (1996). *School size, school climate, and student performance.* Portland, OR: Northwest Regional Educational Laboratory.

Cushman, K. (1996). *Developing curriculum in essential schools. Horace, 12*(4), 1–12.

Davis, D. (2000). *Supporting parent, family, and community involvement in your school.* Portland, OR: Northwest Regional Educational Laboratory. Retrieved December 18, 2006, from http://www.nwrel.org/csrdp/family.pdf

Dianda, M., & McLaren, A. (1996). *A pocket guide to building partnerships for student learning.* Annapolis, MD: National Education Association.

Epstein, J. L., Sanders, M. G., Simon, B. S., Salinas, K. C., Jansorn, N. R., & Van Voorhis, F. L. (2002*). School, family, and community partnerships: Your handbook for action* (2nd ed.). Thousand Oaks, CA: Corwin Press.

Fullan, M. (2001). *The new meaning of educational change* (3rd ed.). New York: Teachers College Press.

Fullan, M., & Hargreaves, A. (1991). *What's worth fighting for: Working together for your school.* Andover, MA: Regional Laboratory of the Northeast and Islands.

Funkhouser, J. E., & Gonzales, M. R. (1997). *Family involvement in children's education: Successful local approaches; An idea book.* Washington, DC: U.S. Department of Education.

Glickman, C. (1993). *Renewing America's schools.* San Francisco: Jossey-Bass.

Hackmann, D. (1997). *Student-led conferences at the middle level.* Champaign, IL: ERIC Clearinghouse on Elementary and Early Childhood Education. (ERIC Digest No. ED407171)

Harvey, S., & Goudvis , A. (2000). *Strategies that work: Teaching comprehension to enhance understanding.* Portland, ME: Stenhouse.

Henderson, A., & Berla, N. (1994). *A new generation of evidence: The family is critical to student achievement.* Washington, DC: Center for Law and Education.

Jackson, A. W., & Davis, G. A. (2000). *Turning Points 2000.* New York: Teachers College Press.

Keene, E. O., & Zimmerman, S. (1997). *Mosaic of thought: Teaching comprehension in a reader's workshop.* Portsmouth, NH: Heinemann.

Levine, D. U., & Lezotte, L. W. (1990). *Unusually effective schools: A review and analysis of research and practice.* Madison, WI: National Center for Effective Schools Research and Development.

Little, J. W. (1990). The persistence of privacy: Autonomy and initiative in teachers' professional relations. *Teachers College Record, 91*(4), 509–536.

McDonald, J. (2001). Students' work and teachers' learning. In A. Lieberman & L. Miller (Eds.), *Teachers caught in the action* (pp. 209–235). New York: Teachers College Press.

Miles-Hawley, K., & Darling-Hammond, L. (1998). Rethinking the allocation of teaching resources: Some lessons from high performing schools. *Educational Evaluation and Policy Analysis, 20*(1), 9–29.

Miles-Hawley, K., & Hornbeck, M. (2000). *Rethinking district professional development spending: New American Schools strategy brief.* Washington, DC: New American Schools.

Murphy, C. (1997). Finding time for faculties to study together. *Journal of Staff Development 18*(3). Retrieved December 19, 2006, from http://64.78.6.92/library/publications/jsd/murphy183.cfm

Neufeld, B. (1999). *Evaluation report for Boston Plan for Excellence.* Cambridge, MA: Education Matters.

Newmann, F., & Wehlage, G. (1995). *Successful school restructuring.* Madison, WI: Center on Organization and Restructuring of Schools.

Oakes, J. (1985). *Keeping track: How schools structure inequality.* New Haven, CT: Yale University Press.

Poliner, R., & Lieber, C. M. (2004). *The advisory guide.* Cambridge, MA: Educators for Social Responsibility.

Rugen, L. (1995). The one-day community exploration: An expeditionary learning professional development experience. In E. Cousins & M. Rodgers (Eds.), *Fieldwork: Vol. 1.* Dubuque, IA: Kendall/Hunt.

Steinberg, A., & Allen, L. (2002). *From large to small: Strategies for personalizing the high school.* Boston: Jobs for the Future.

Stiefel, L., Berne, R., Iatarola, P., & Frutcher, N. (2000). High school size: Effects on budgets and performance in New York City. *Educational Evaluation and Policy Analysis, 22*(1), 27–39.

Tomlinson, C. A. (1995). *The differentiated classroom.* Alexandria, VA: Association for Supervision and Curriculum Development.

Wheelock, A. (1992). *Crossing the tracks: How "untracking" can save America's schools.* New York: New Press.

Wiggins, G., & McTighe, J. (2001). *Understanding by design.* Alexandra, VA: Association for Supervision and Curriculum Development.

Index

CORWIN PRESS

The Corwin Press logo—a raven striding across an open book—represents the union of courage and learning. Corwin Press is committed to improving education for all learners by publishing books and other professional development resources for those serving the field of PreK–12 education. By providing practical, hands-on materials, Corwin Press continues to carry out the promise of its motto: **"Helping Educators Do Their Work Better."**

27/2 Gift